Unicorns, Mermaids, Dragons and More!

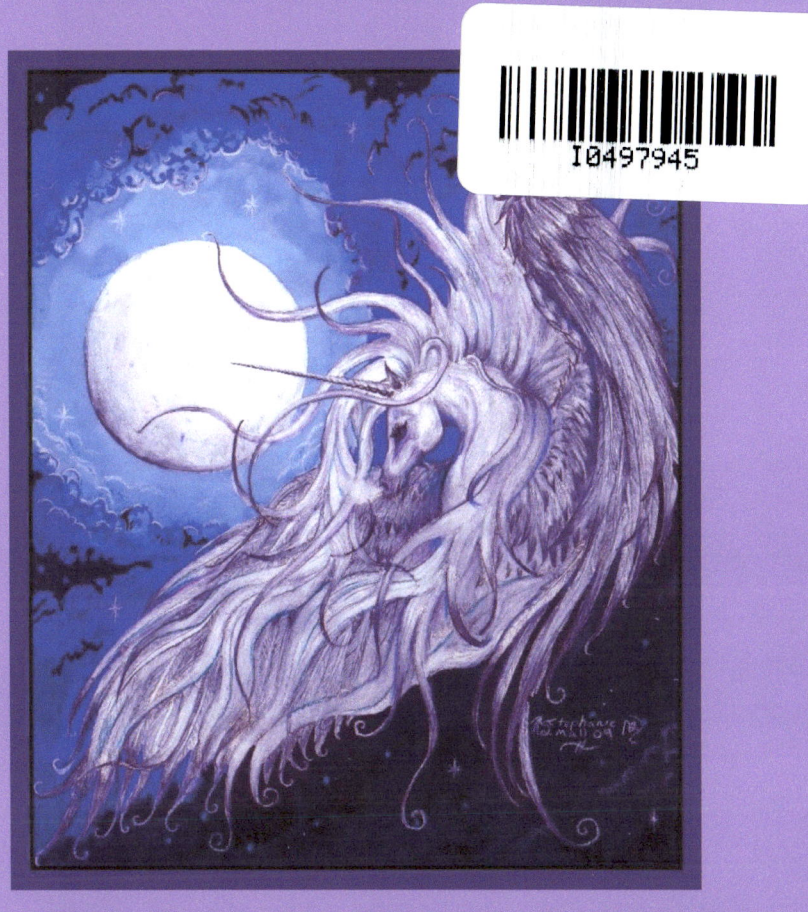

The Fantasy Art of Stephanie Small

Unicorns, Mermaids, Dragons and More

The Fantasy Art of Stephanie Small

Tir'Rielle Publishing / Clip Clop Workshop

Copyright © 2018 by Stephanie Small

All rights reserved. This book or any portion thereof may not be reproduced or used in any manner whatsoever without the express written permission of the publisher except for the use of brief quotations in a book review or scholarly journal.

ISBN-13: 978-1721651931

ISBN-10: 1721651934

First Printing: 2018

Clip Clop Workshop

Tir'Rielle Publishing

Vallejo, CA 94590

www.clipclopworkshop.com

Have you ever felt drawn to magic? Do you see magic in nature? Do you look at the colors and feel like recording them? Perhaps you have an artist's mind and art. Even if you are not an artist you too can engage your creative side.

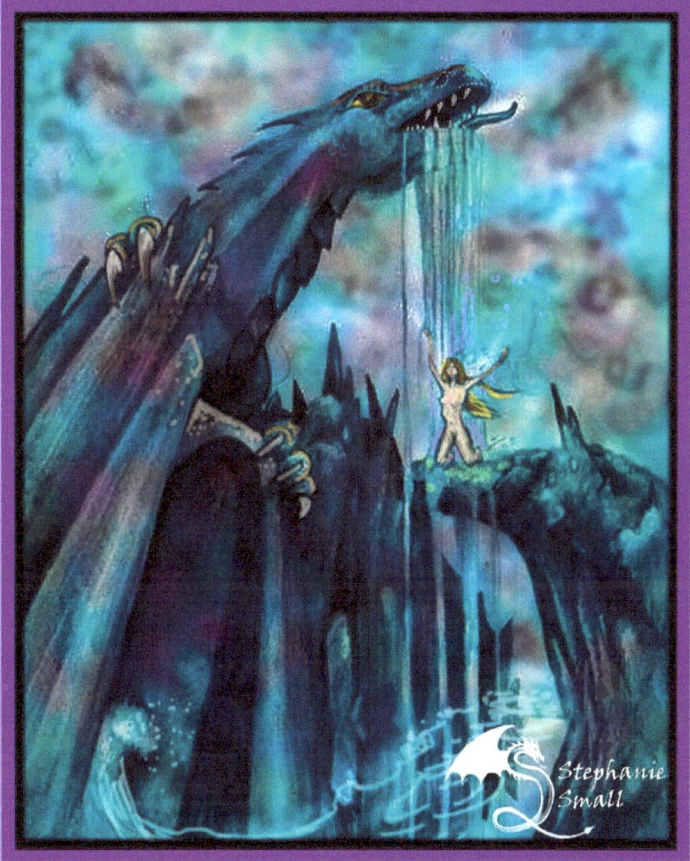

The image above I started in High School and colored 20 years later. I was going to St. Helena High School in the Napa Valley. I had grown u in California and Oregon. I had an early interest in nature and animals that would influence my artistic and scholastic endeavors. I felt drawn to magic, to dragons, to the ocean and to color.

My mom would take us to the Oregon Zoo regularly. I would gain a familiarity and confidence with animal anatomy. Looking at exotic zoo animals was inspiring.

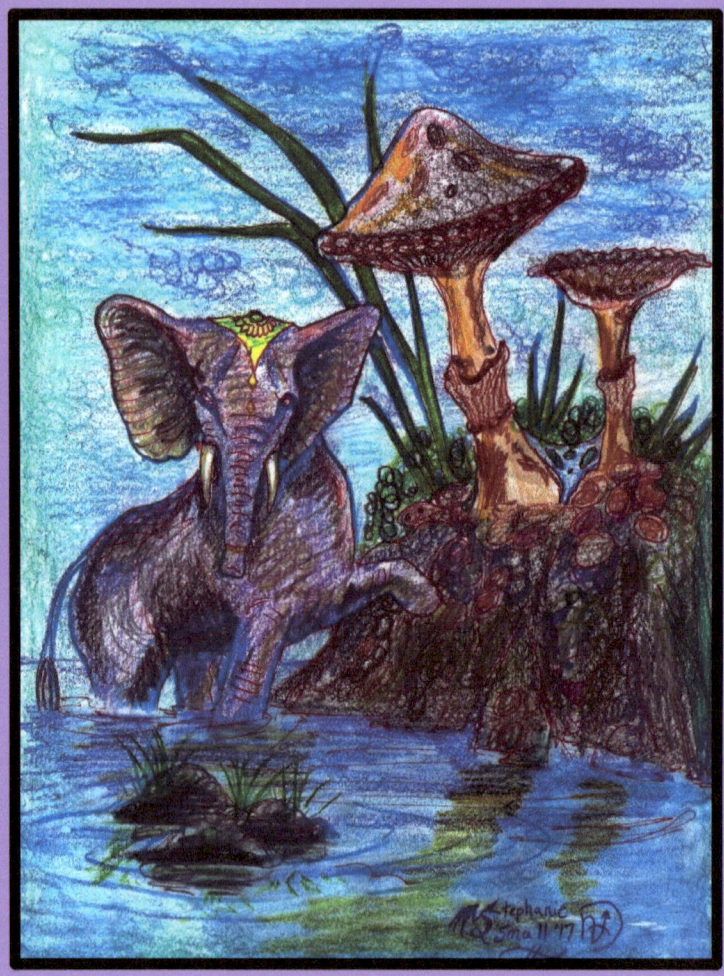

Early on I got to handle animals which lead to internships with veterinary clinics, shelters and stables. I was raised on a farm. This gave me the opportunity to see and handle animals up close. Seeing them in action allowed me to better understand how to draw them.

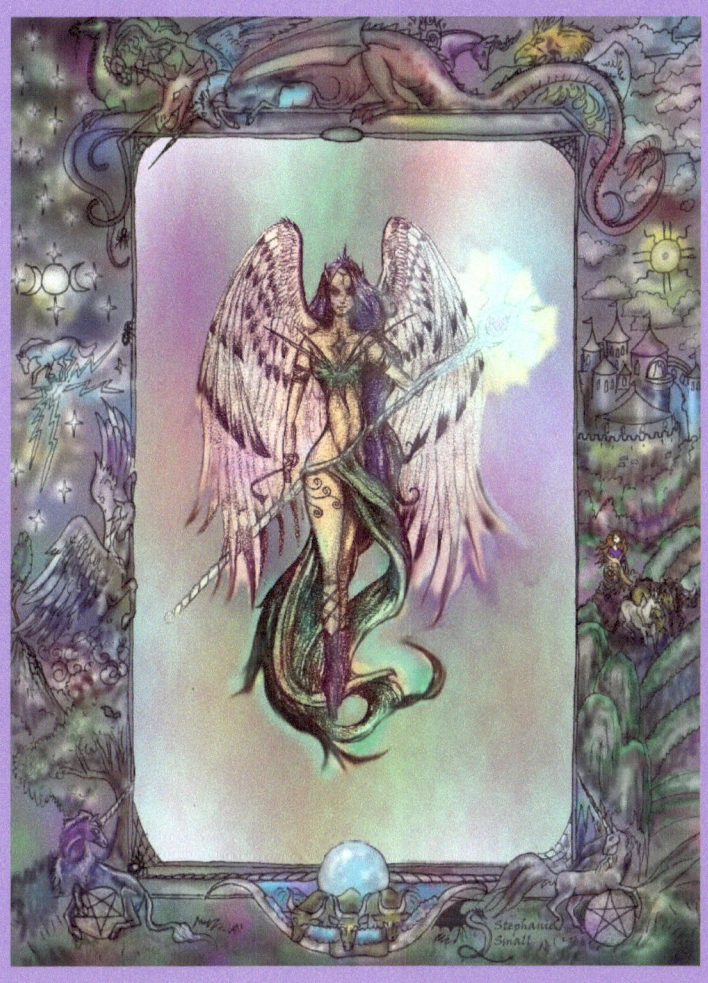

Spirituality is important to me. Drawing from mythology, lore and metaphysical learning, I design unique art inspired by ancient knowledge.

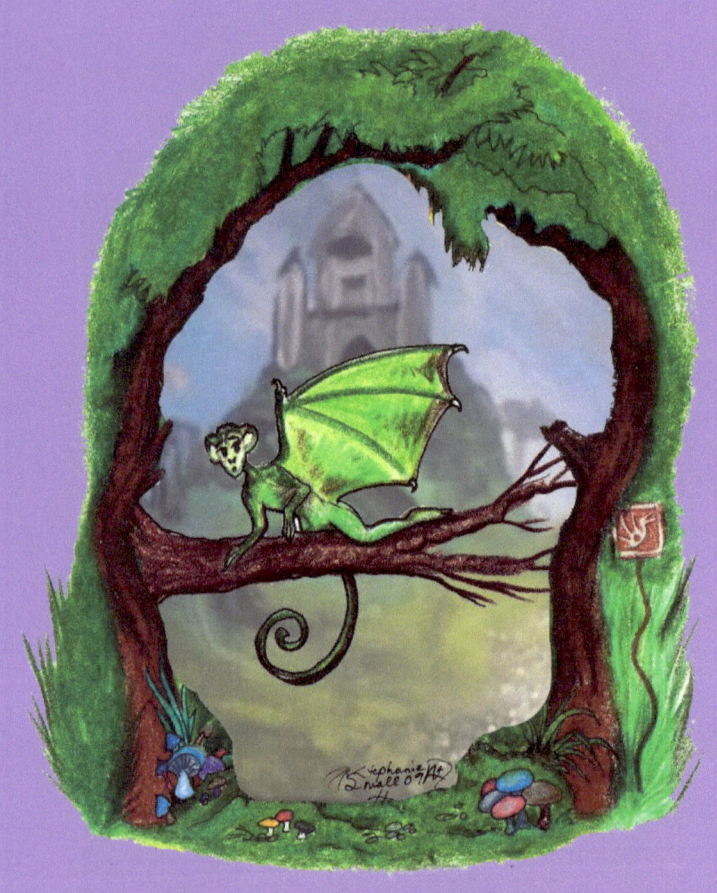

In Napa Valley, there are rumors of rebobs, flying monkeys that are said to reside in the Forests. I have always loved our local legend and draw it often.

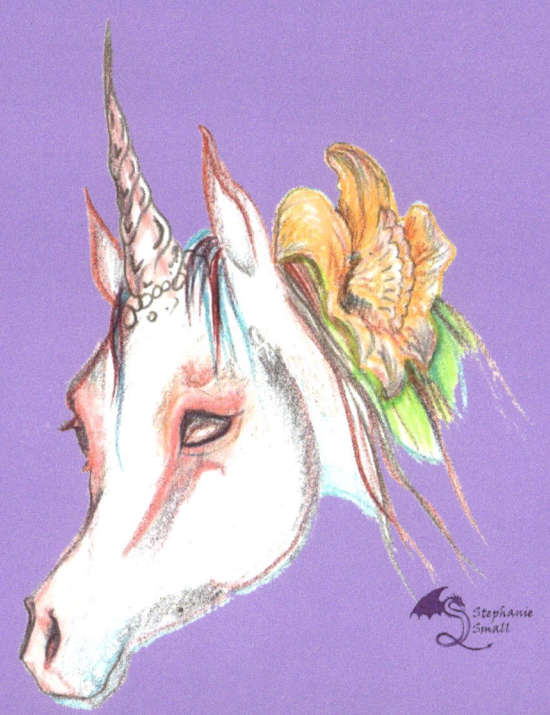
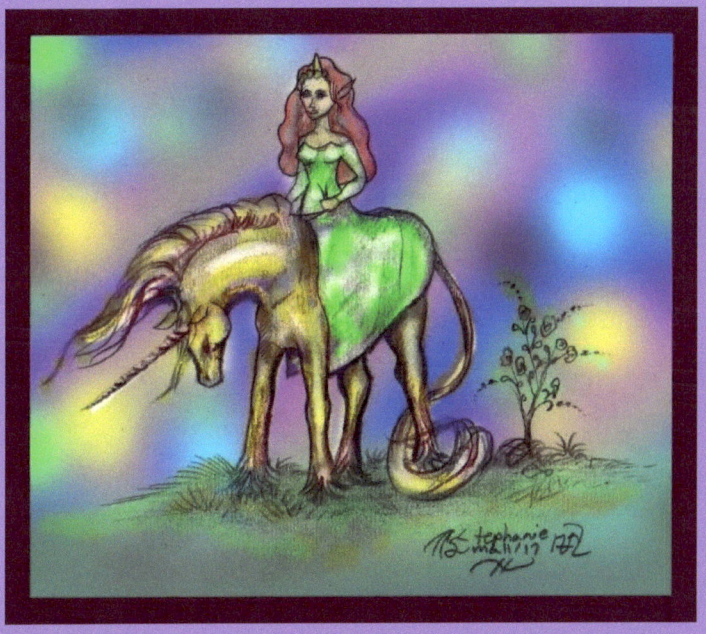

The dynamic dragon is a complementary creature to the healing unicorn. To me they are a beautiful union of two ideal beings.

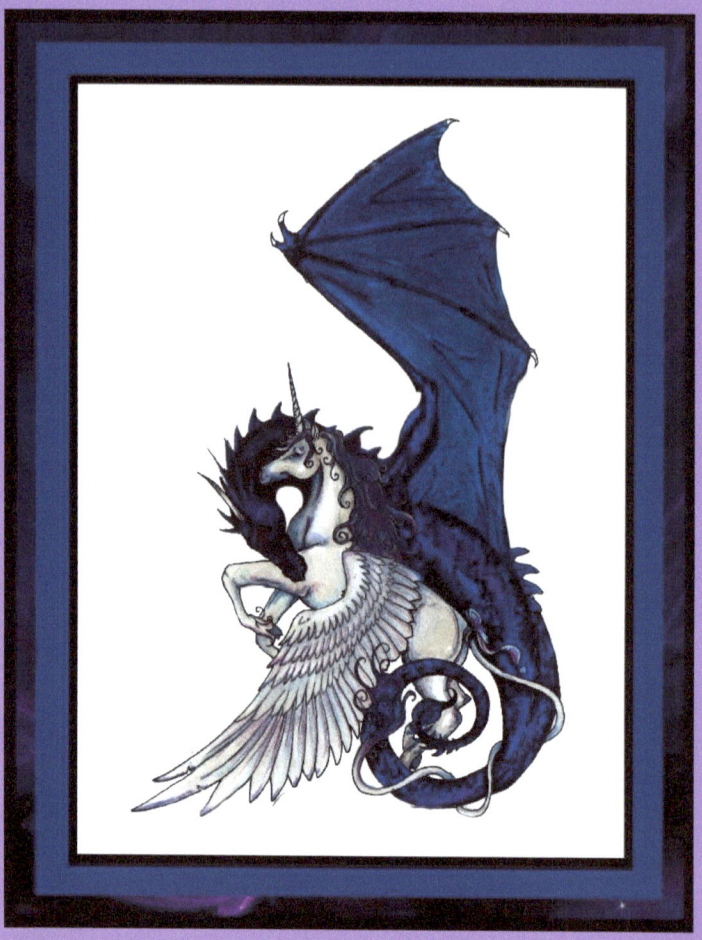

Mythology, heraldry and other lore have influenced my art. I love the symbolism of creatures and magical beings.

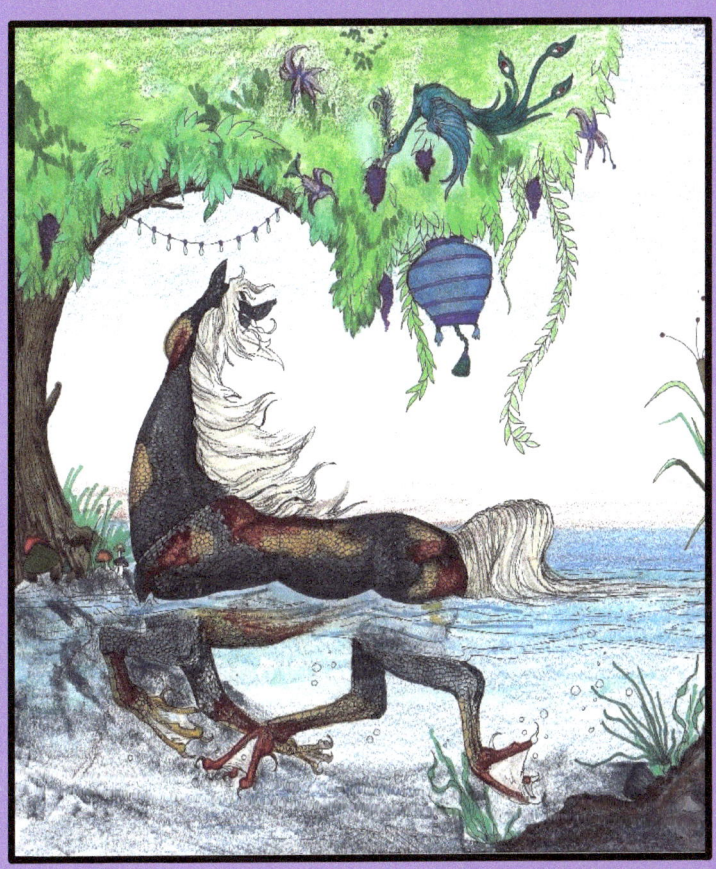

Mixing together multiple types of creatures can allow you to explore the boundaries of your imagination. Sometimes, simply choosing a few rare and unique creatures to merge can create fun hybrids. Through innovation, new creatures can be imagined.

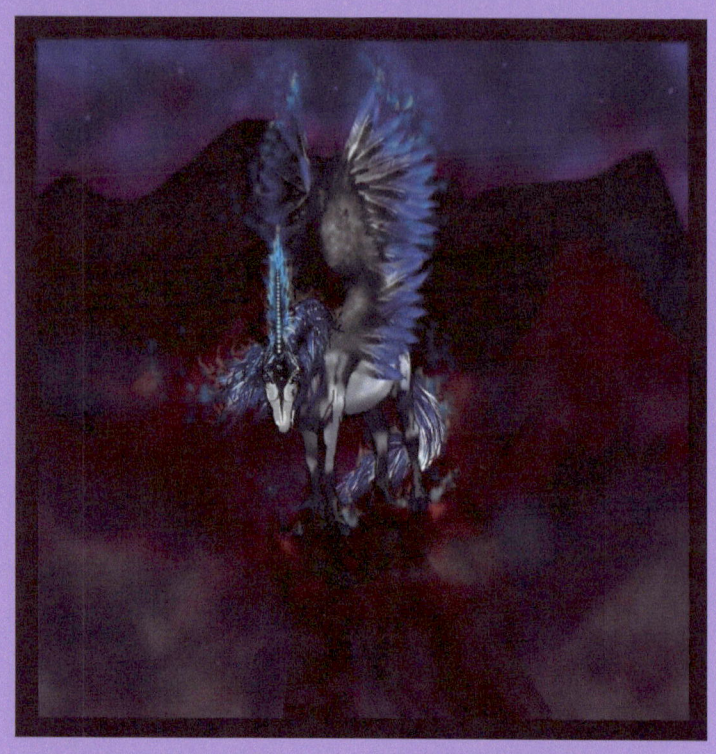
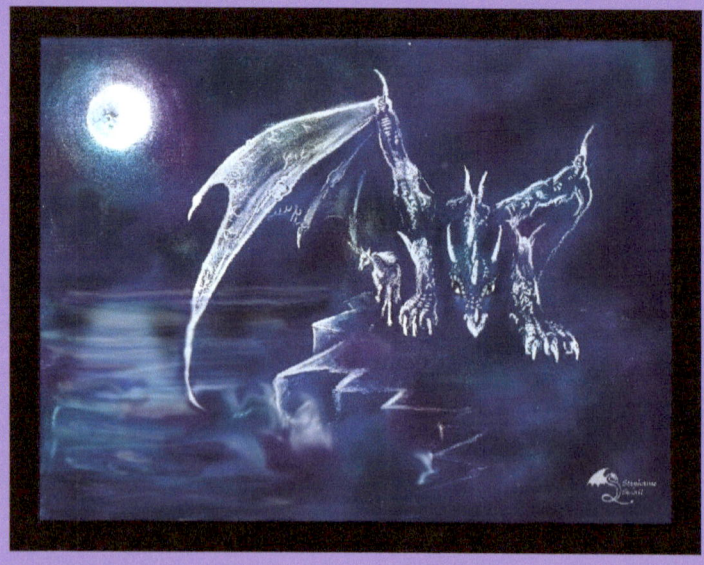

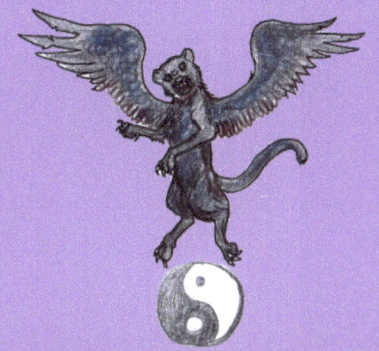

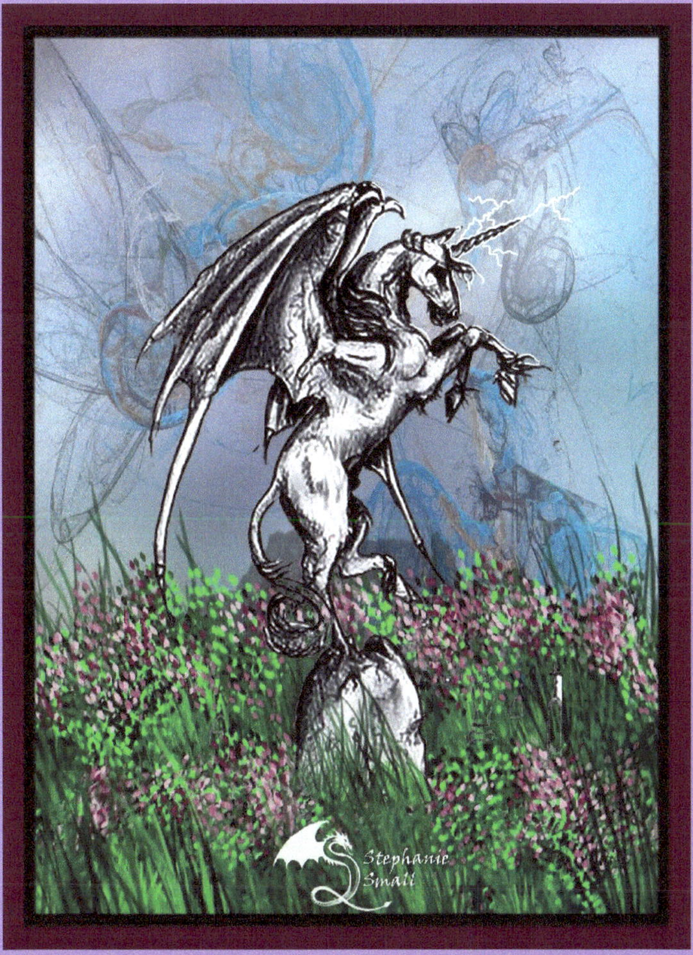

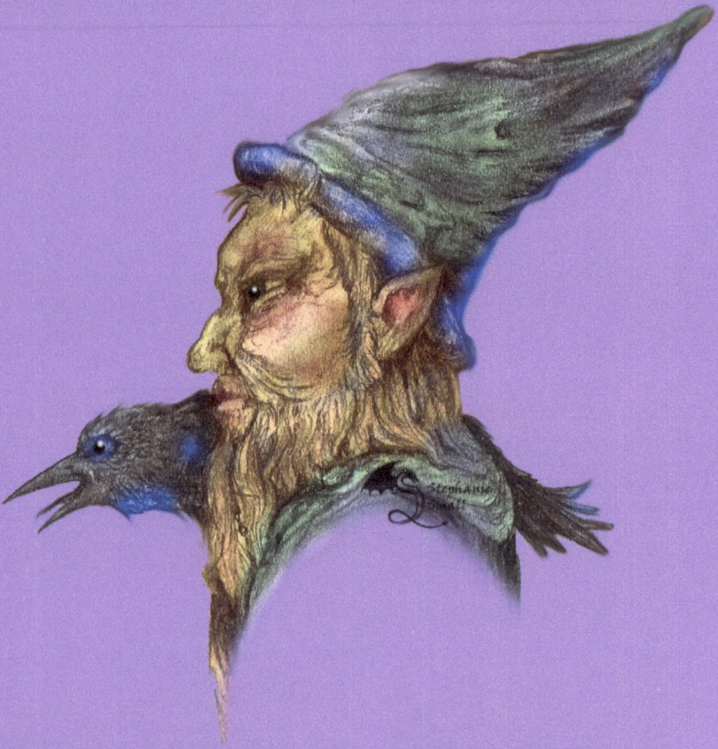

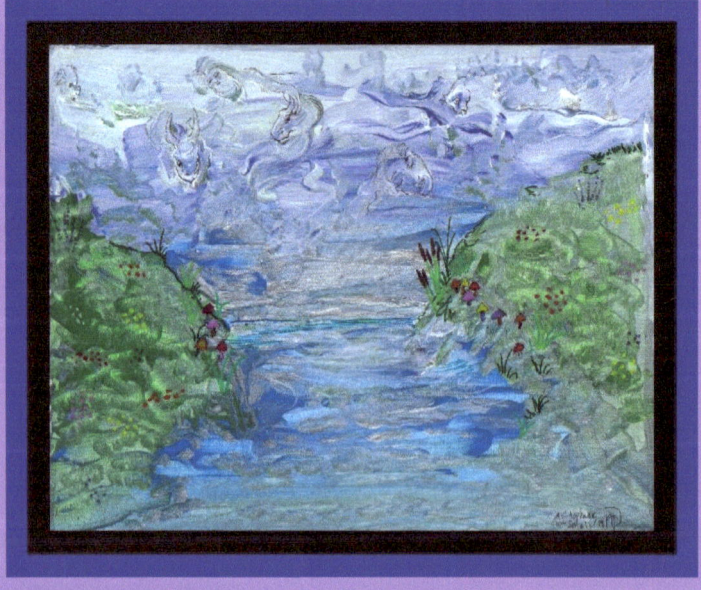

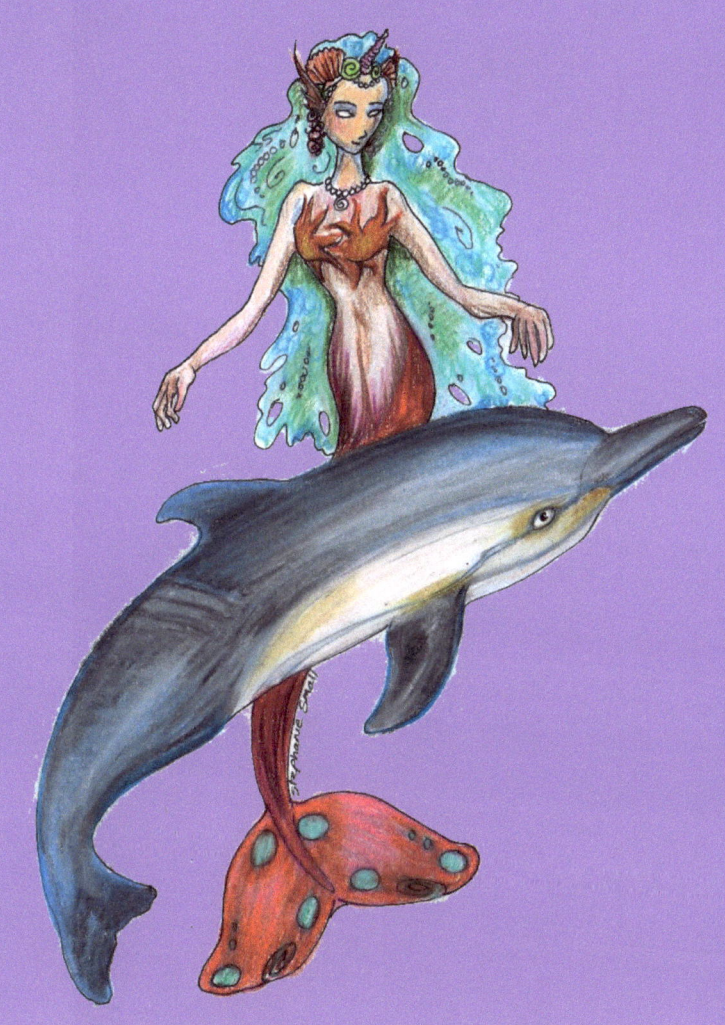

Mermaids are magical beings from the water. It is said they have beautiful voices. Some legends say mermen, their male counterparts are not as lovely looking. They are known for their fishlike tails and long hair. Some people believe they were inspired by manatees.

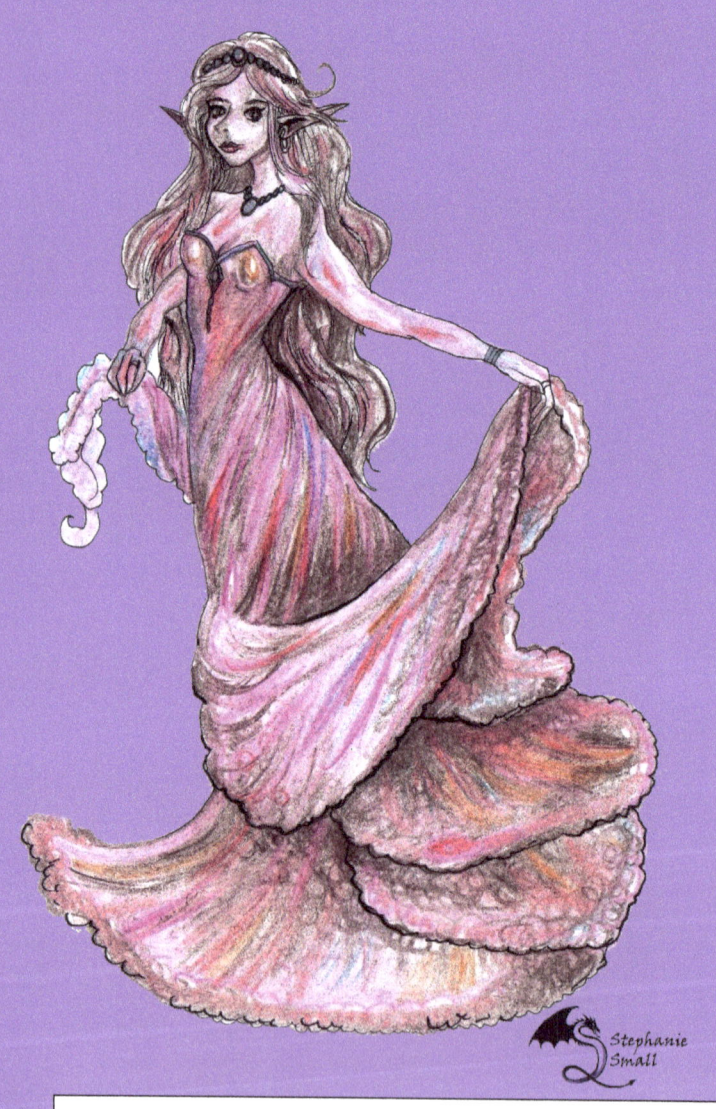

Elves are fantastic creatures with a kinship to nature. They can be very tall or even very short. Elf stories are told worldwide and they are considered guardians of nature.

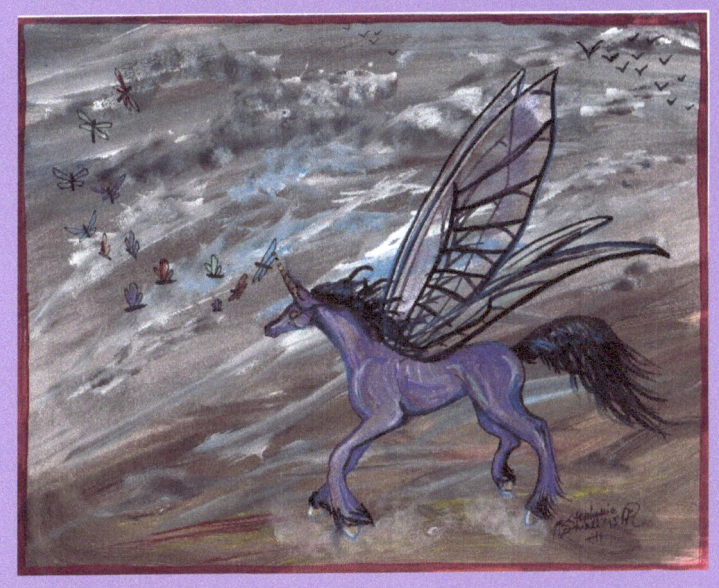
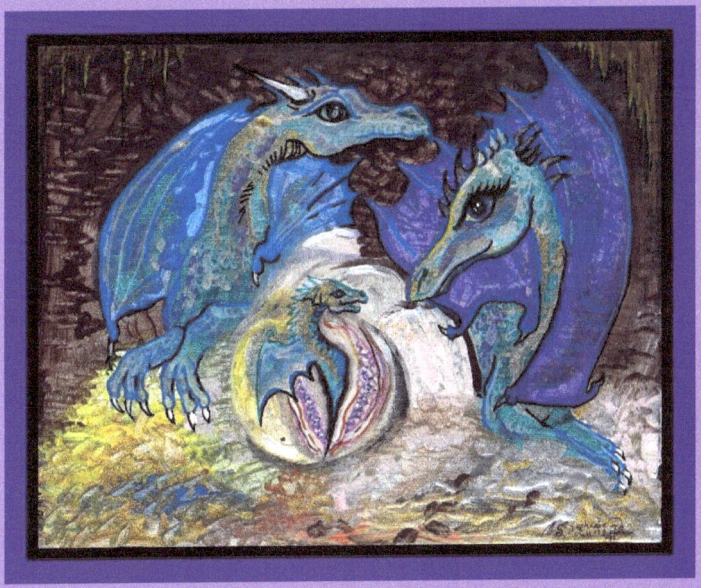

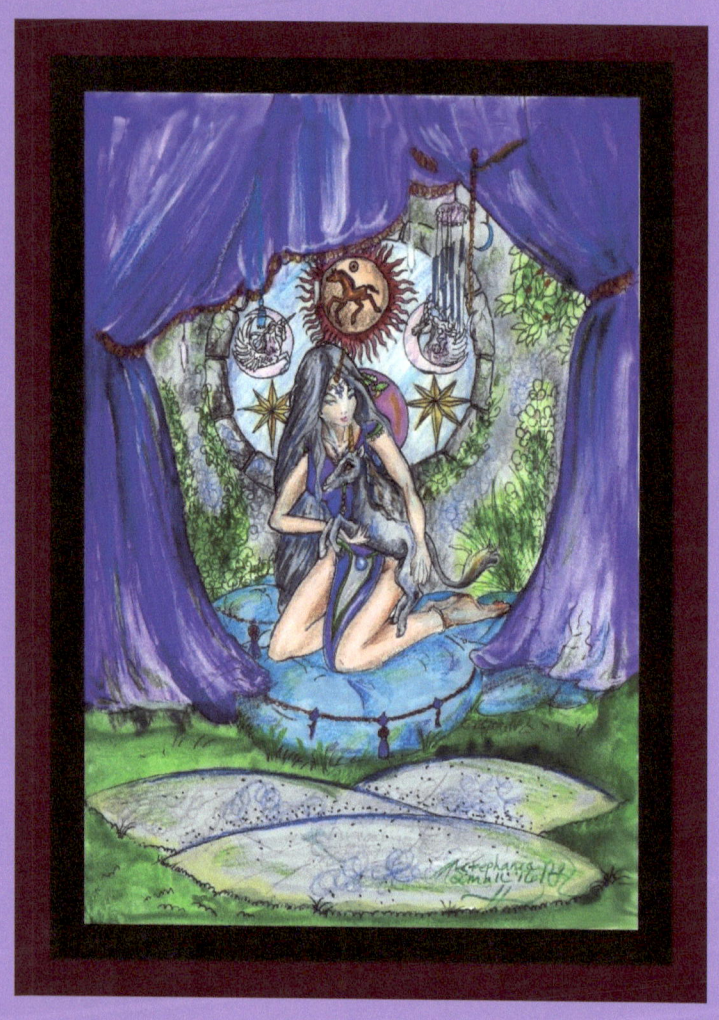

Some pieces are inspired by dreams. I keep a dream journal to record unique dream experiences. Later, those dreams can be translated into art. Sometimes I draw a piece many years later.

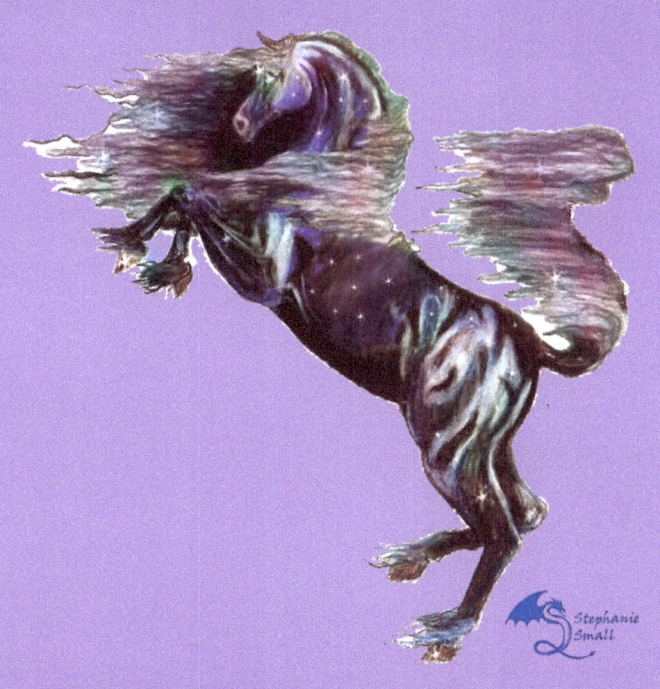
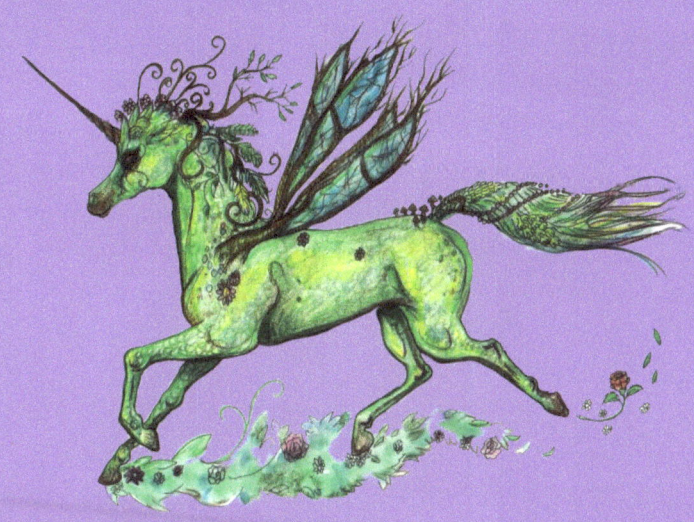

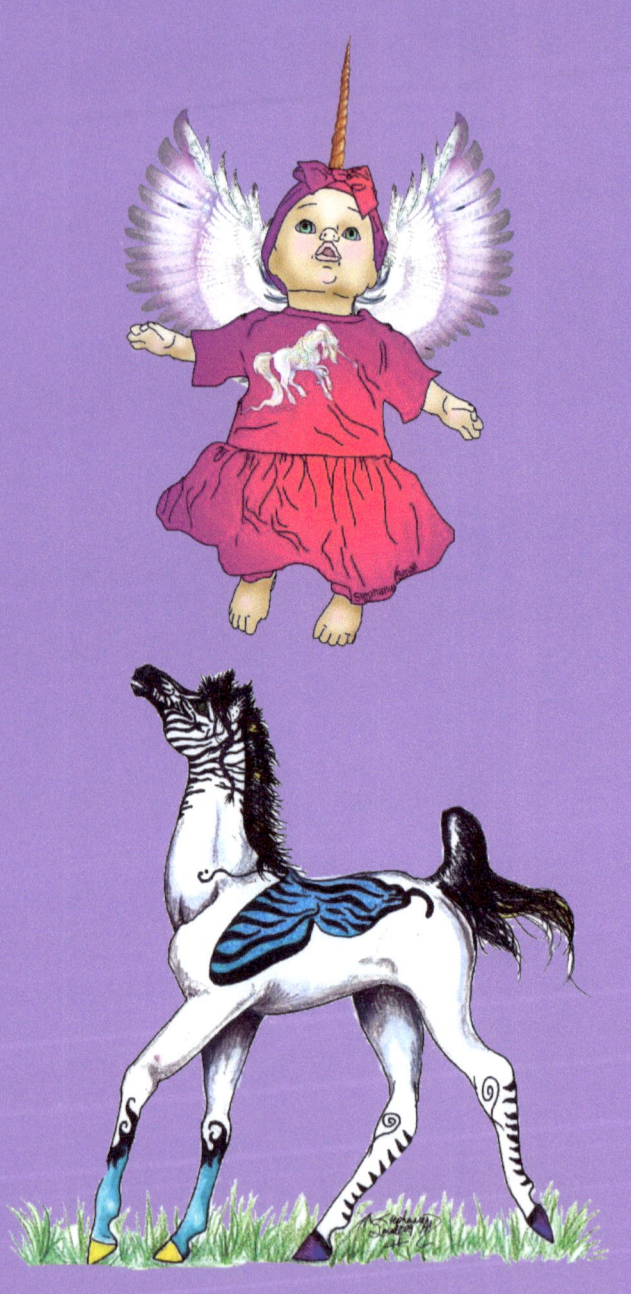

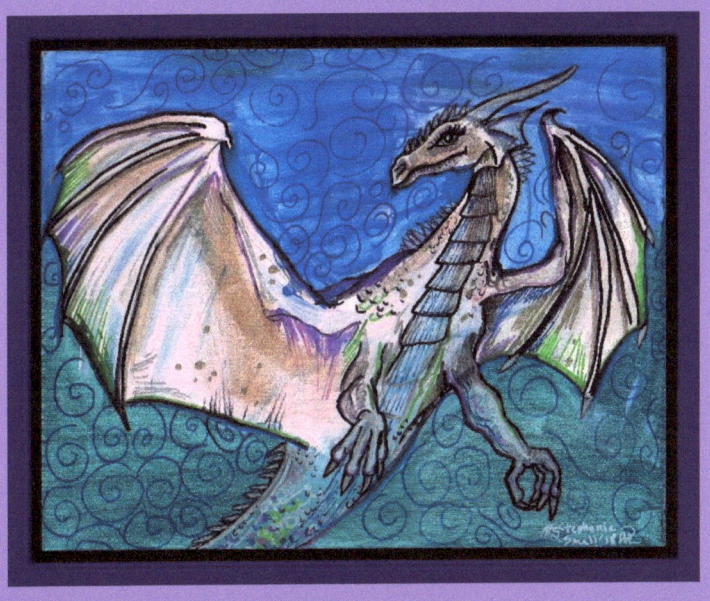
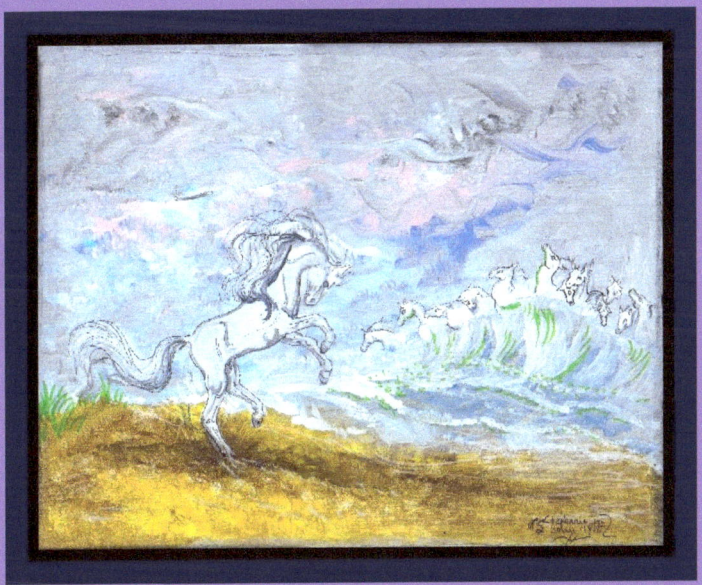

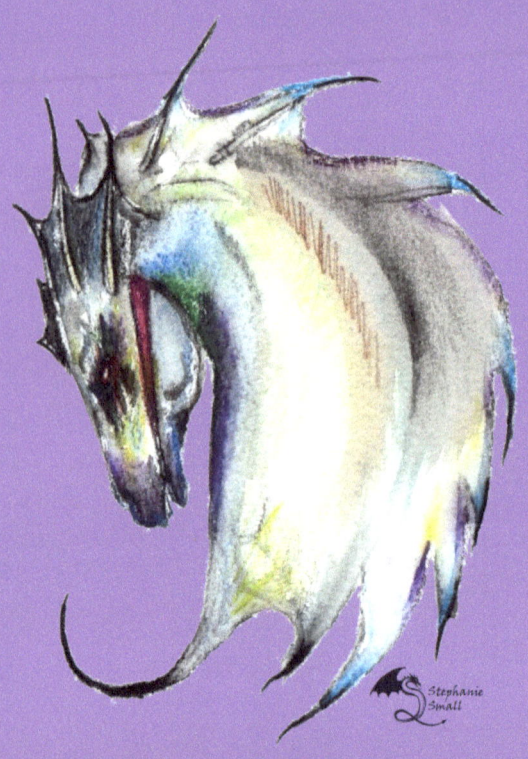
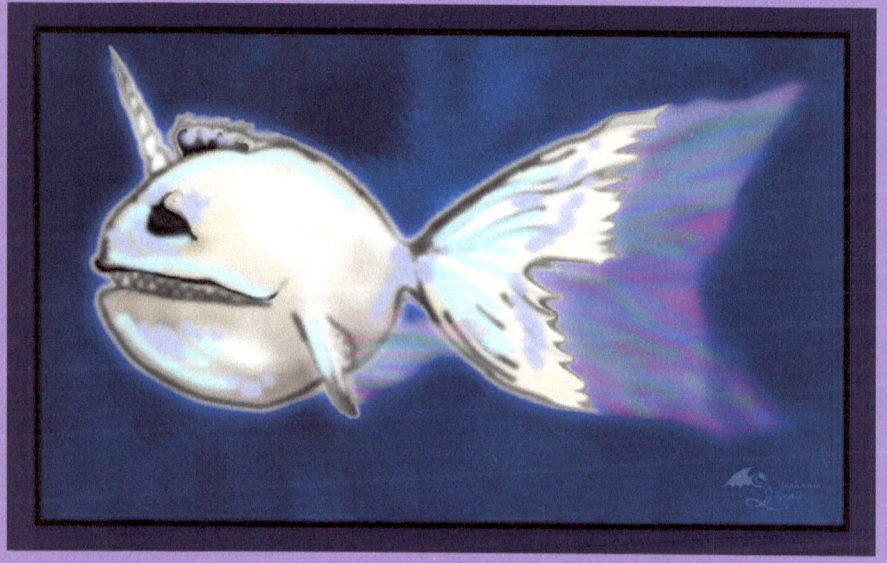

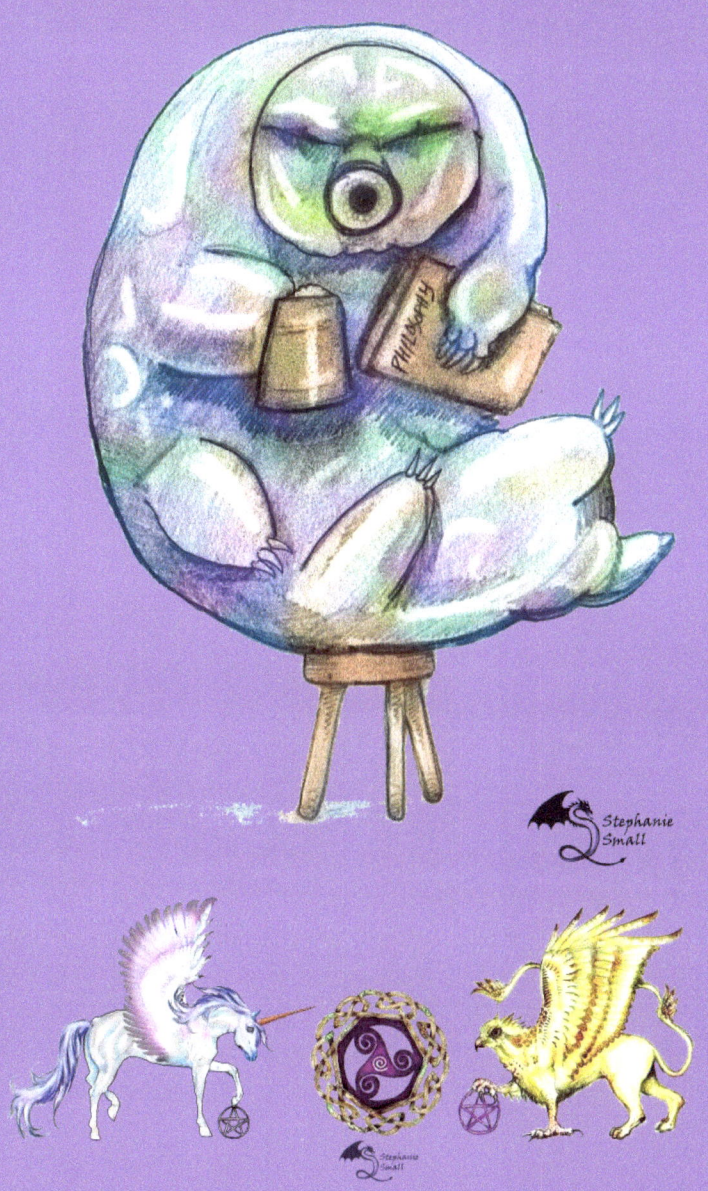

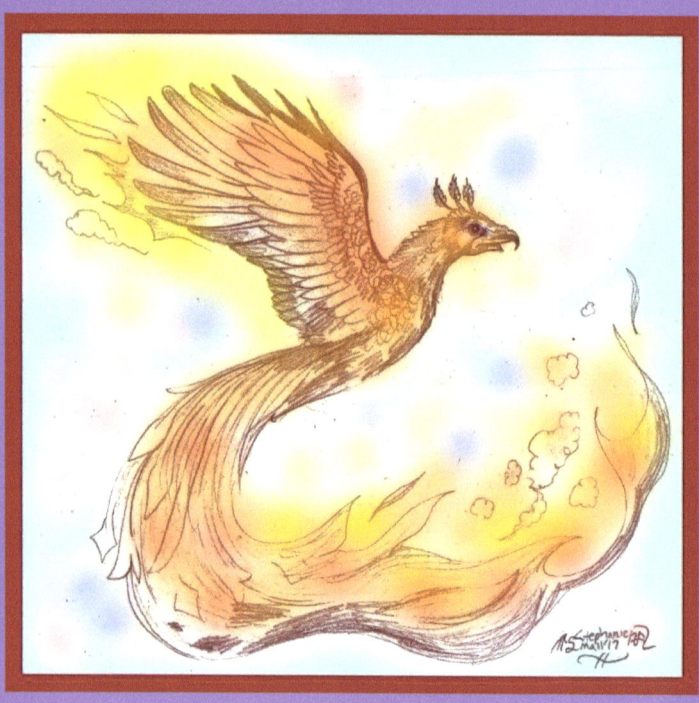

The phoenix bird has a powerful association with fire. It is said to be a noble bird that lives forever. It renews itself by building a nest in a palm tree. It will then adorn itself with incense. Once arranged, the bird will then set fire to the tree. The bird will then burn up and in its place is an egg. The egg hatches, and it is the phoenix reborn. Phoenix lore is ancient, and it is recognized in many parts of the world. People see the phoenix as a symbol of rebirth, renewal and regeneration. They are said to have healing powers and are often pictured with a long, flaming tail.

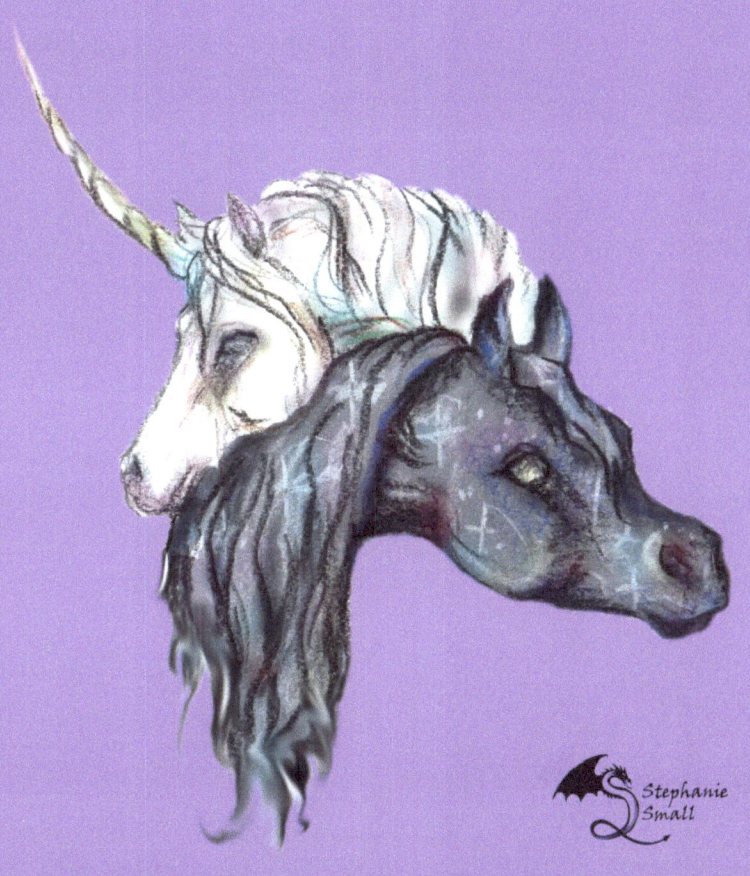

I love unicorns and horses. Much of drawing them is recognizing how they move and where their feet will be placed. Unicorns are known for their long horn and healing powers. There are also winged horses. Though the name of a specific winged horse was Pegasus, this is often the term used to refer to winged horses. Horse lore is prevalent through human history.

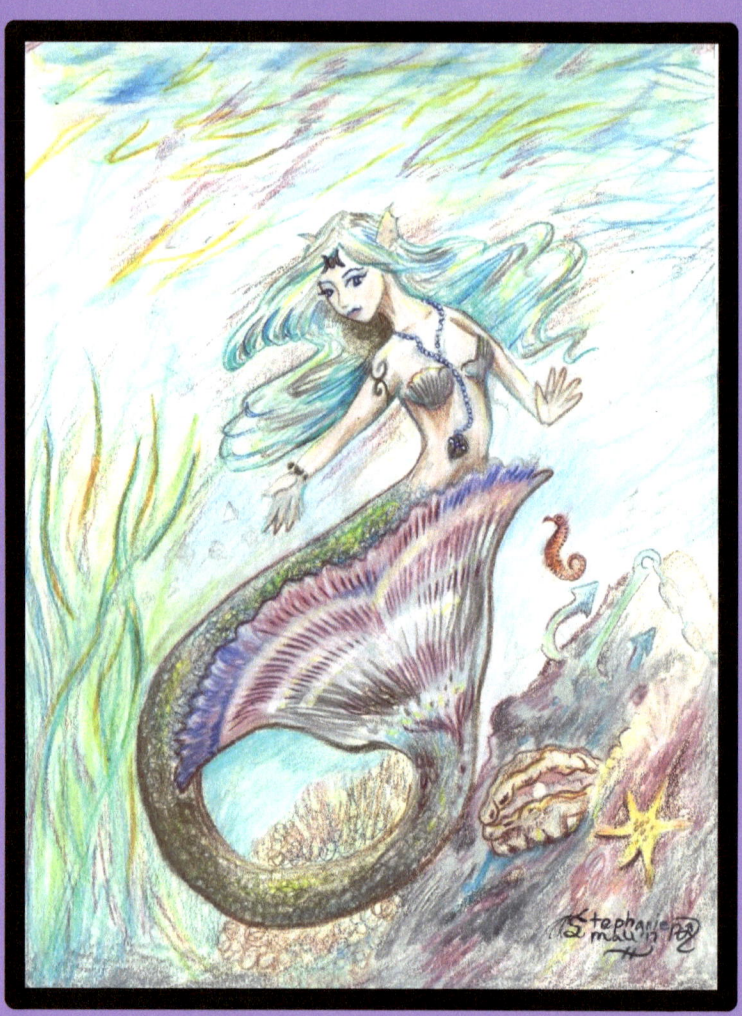

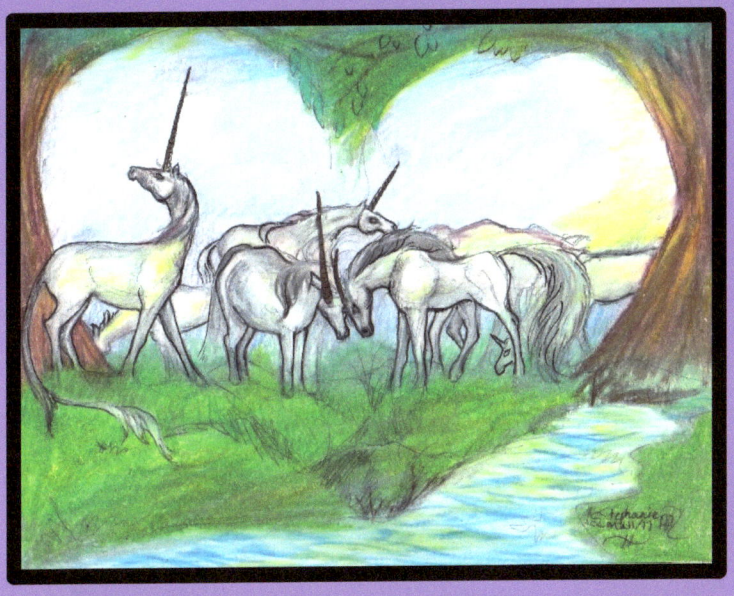
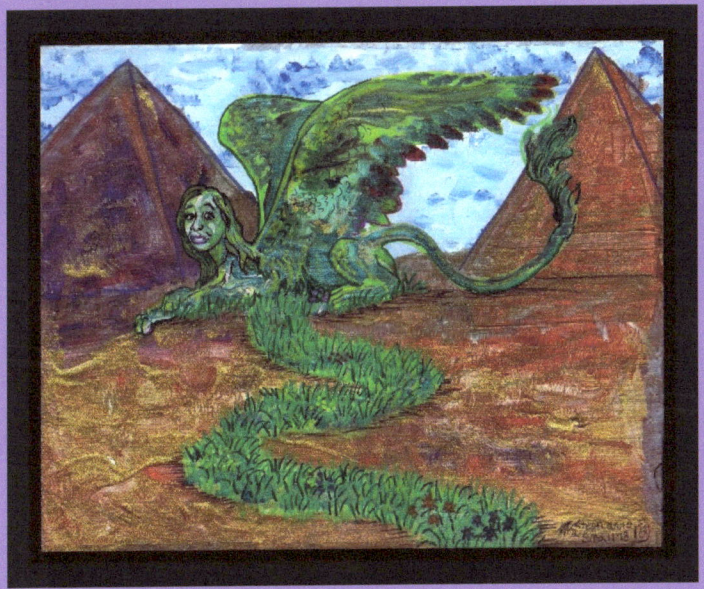

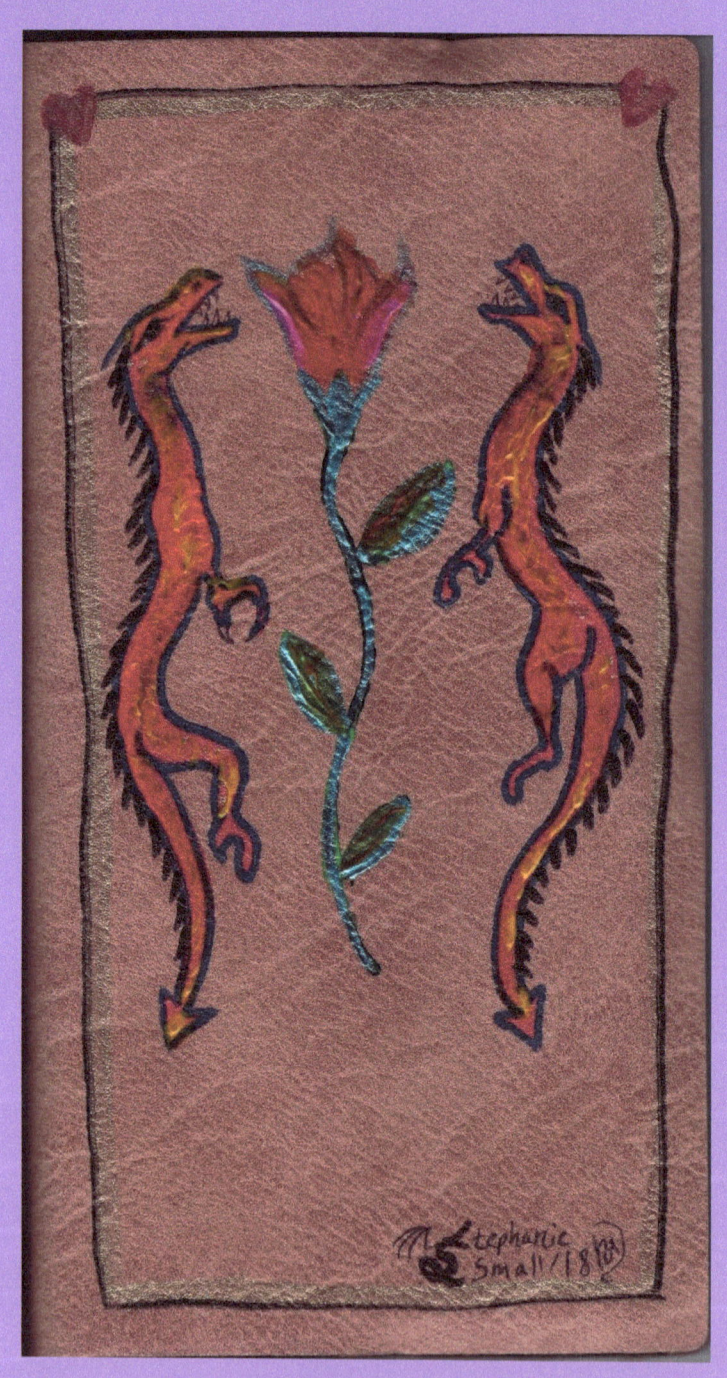

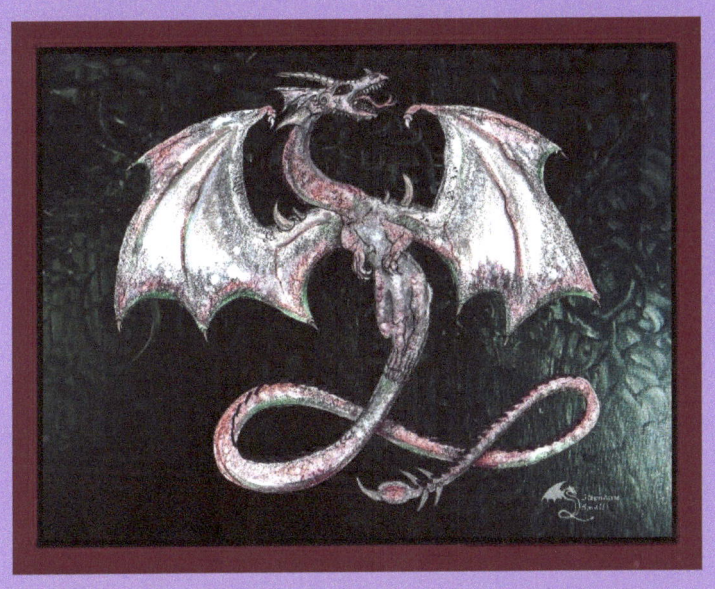
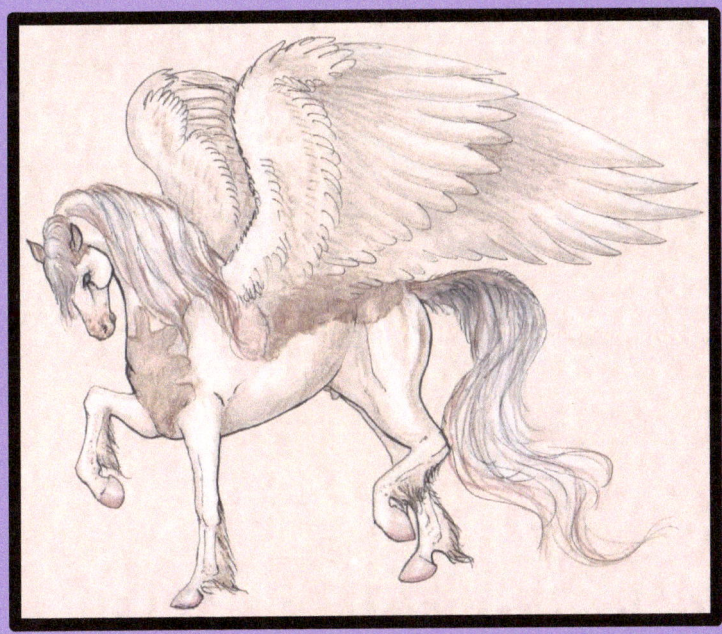

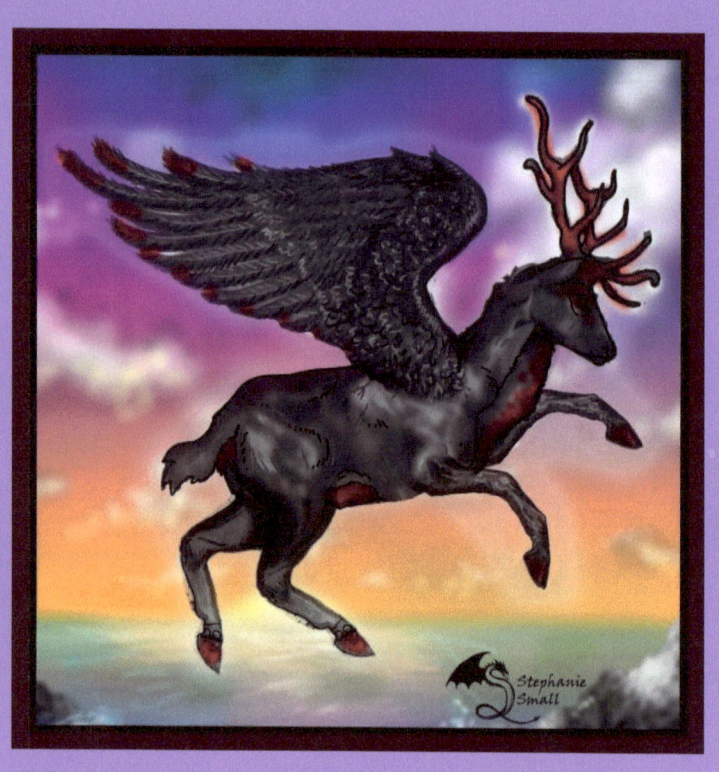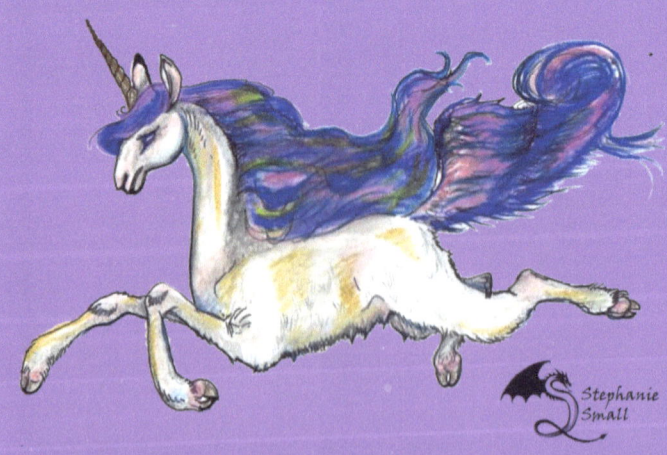

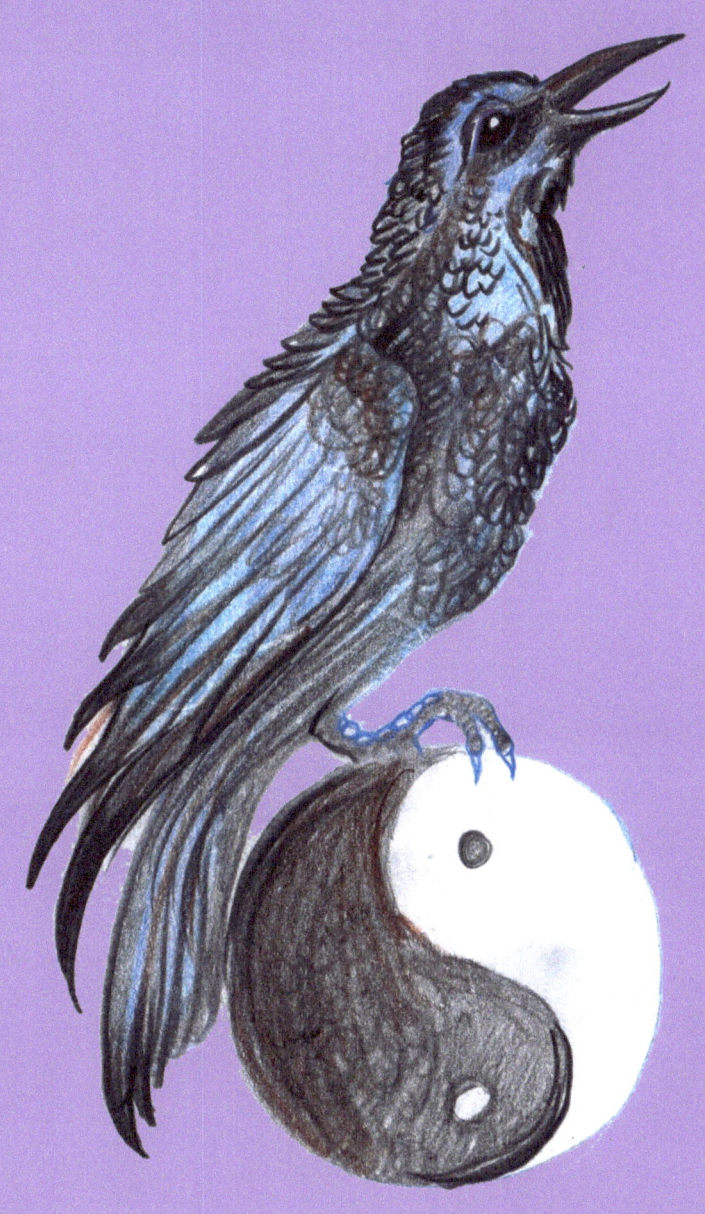

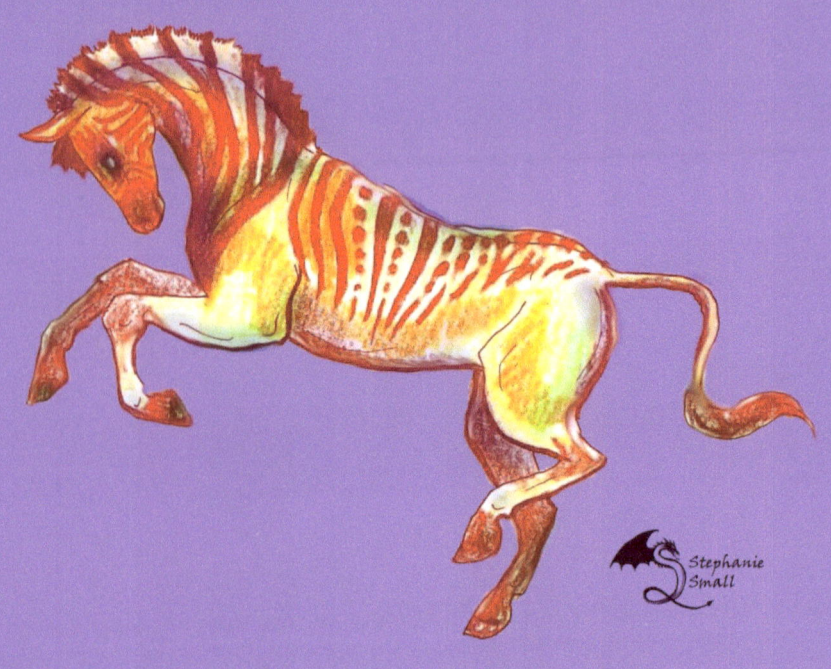

I love zebras. I used to observe them and draw them at the zoo. Once, I bottlefed a zebra. There are several species of zebra. They are all quite wild and refuse to be domesticated. Unlike horses, zebras are more aggressive and to protect themselves from lions and other predators.

Though they do not show up in the crazy colors above, zebra patterns are unique and each one is like a fingerprint. No two zebras look quite the same. It is said the stripes help protect them from predators by making it hard to tell one zebra from another. Also, some flies are confused by the zebra pattern and are less likely to bite the zebra.

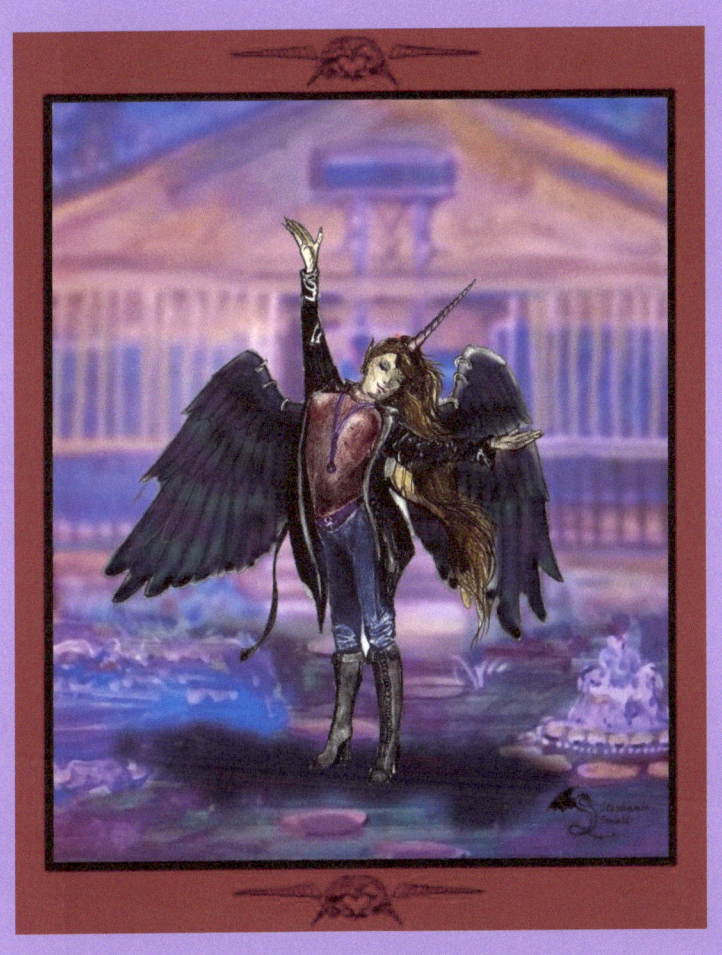

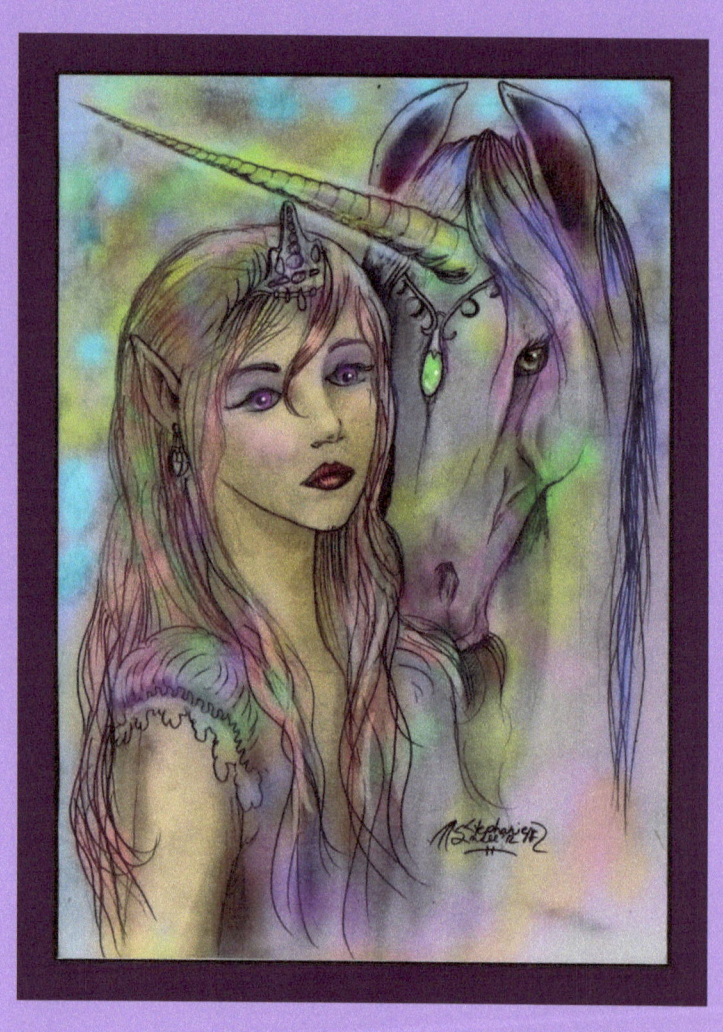

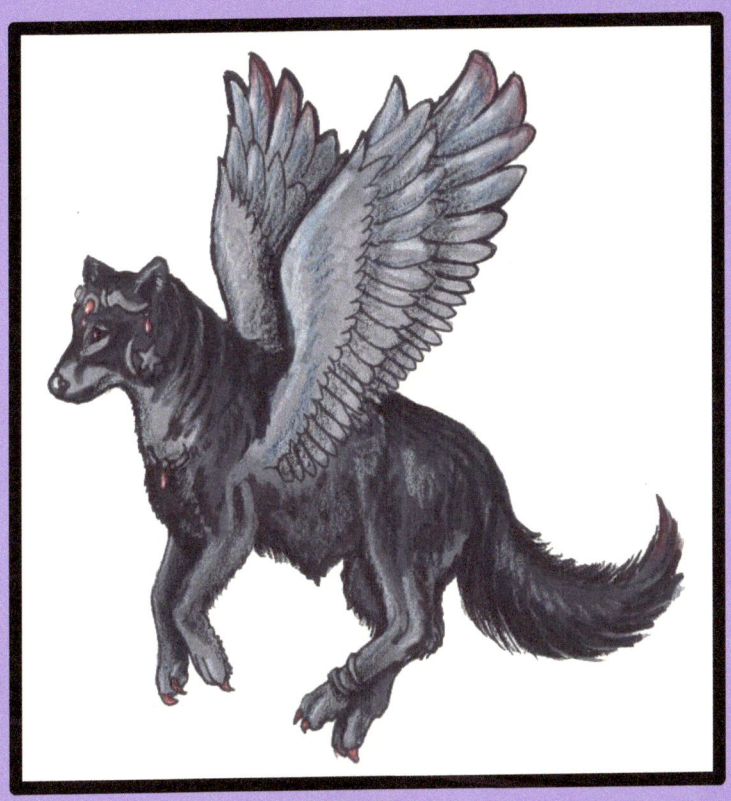

Wolves are fantastic beings that can survive harsh conditions. They have great endurance and can run long distances. They hunt and live in packs which have very strict structures. Wolves are becoming very rare and are extinct in some locations.

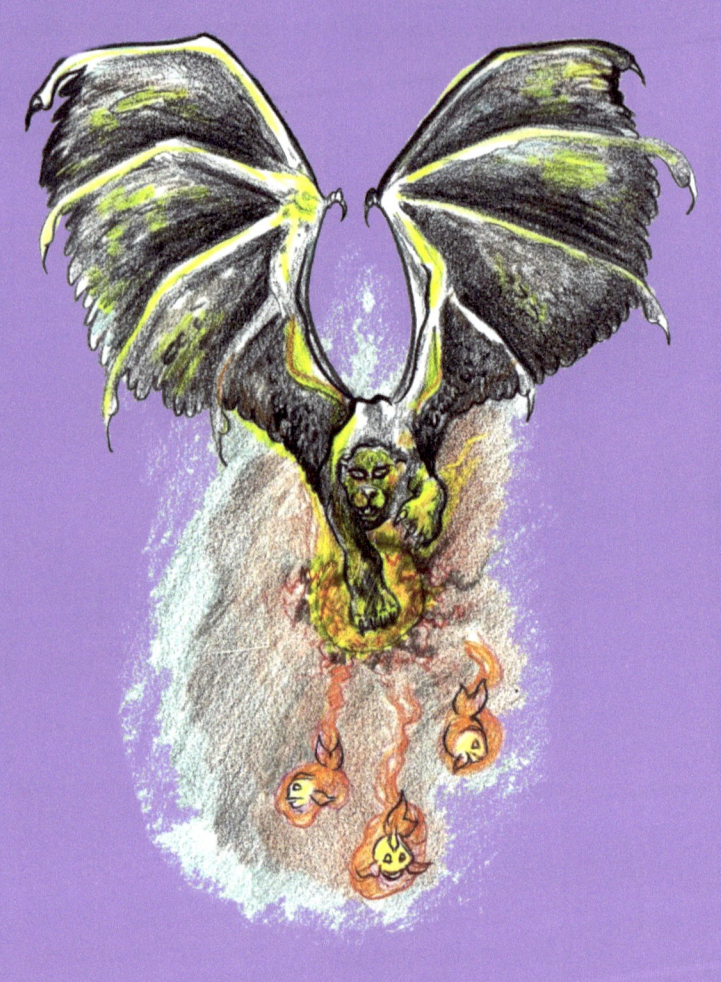

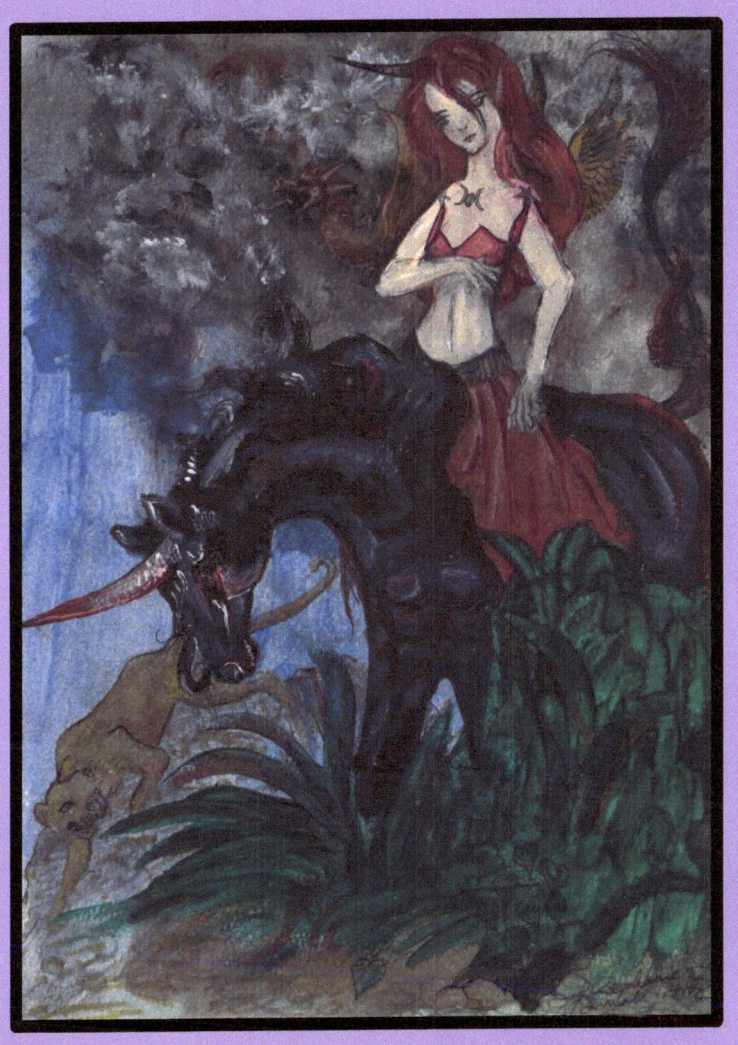

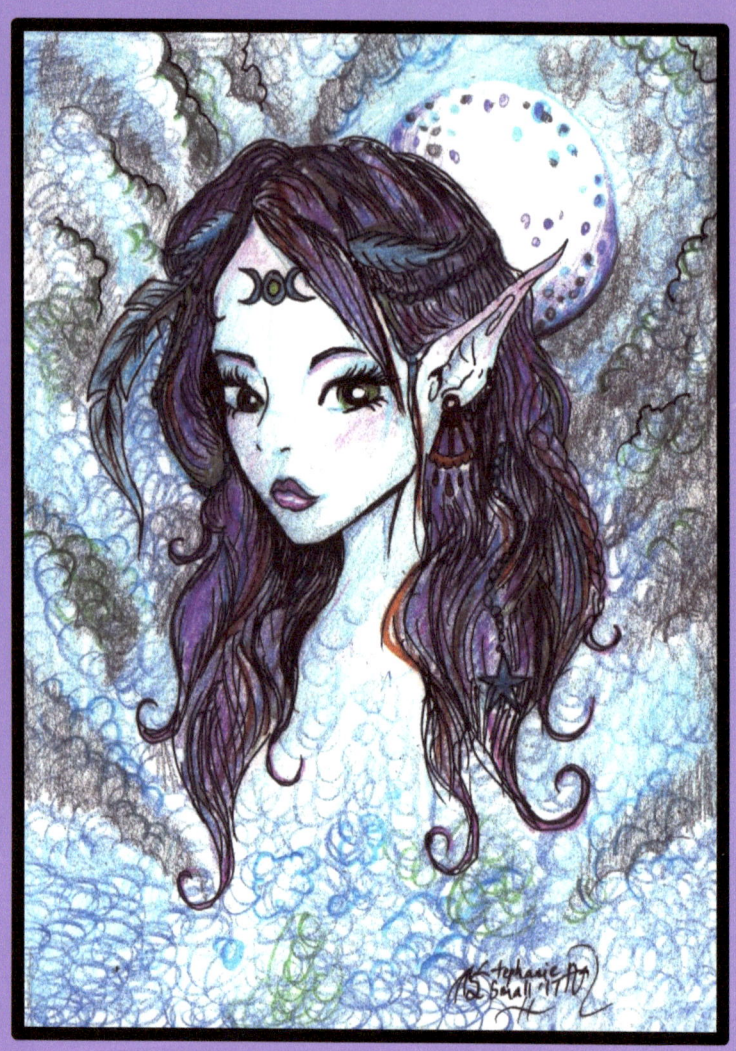

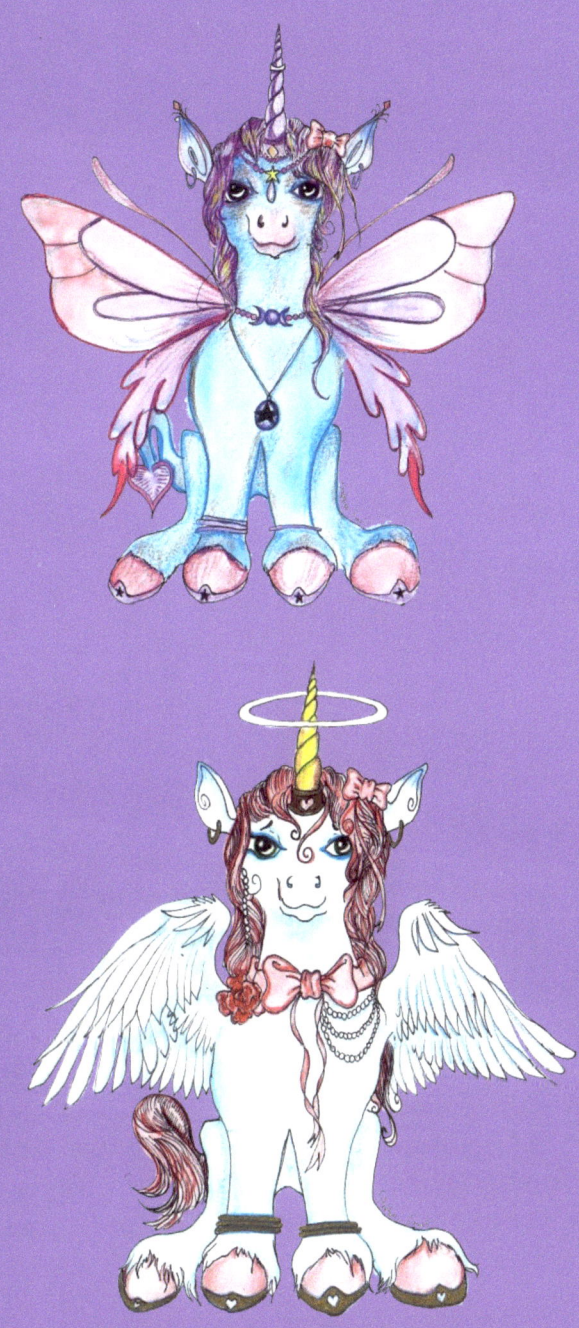

Art by Stephanie Small

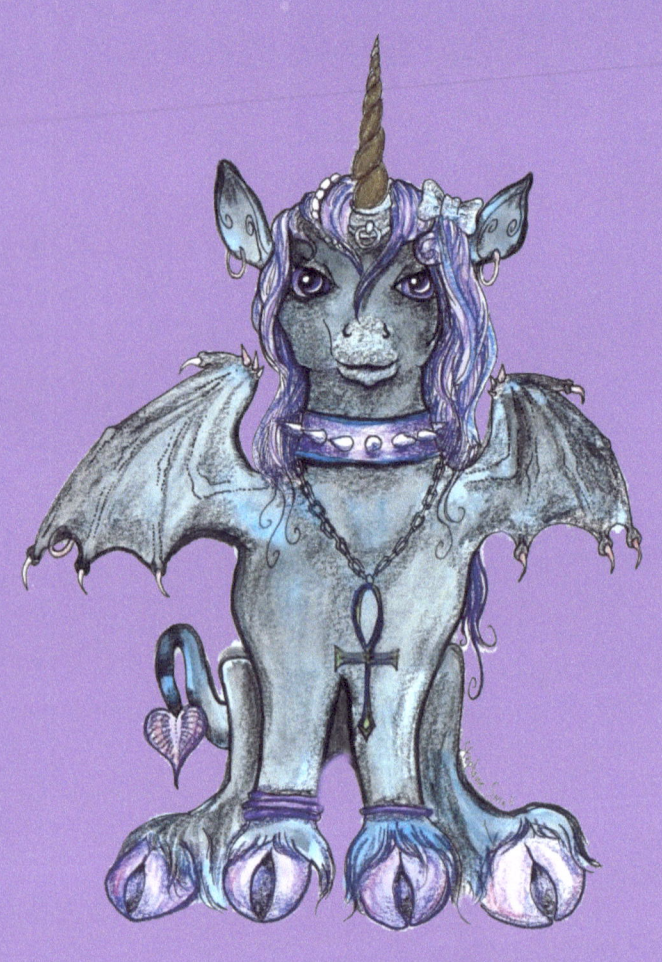

I always feel like a unicorn but sometimes I feel like different kinds of unicorns. I designed these unique-corns which are unicorn-hybrids of fairy, angel, goth, dragon or lion.

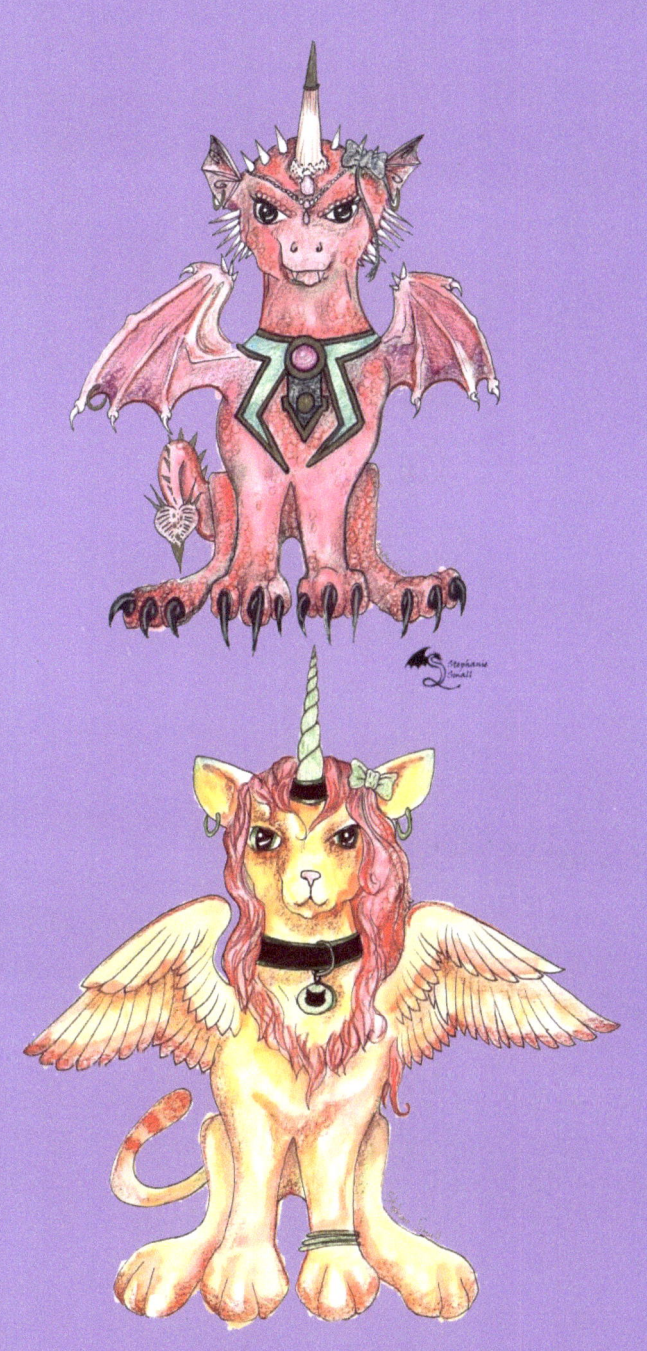

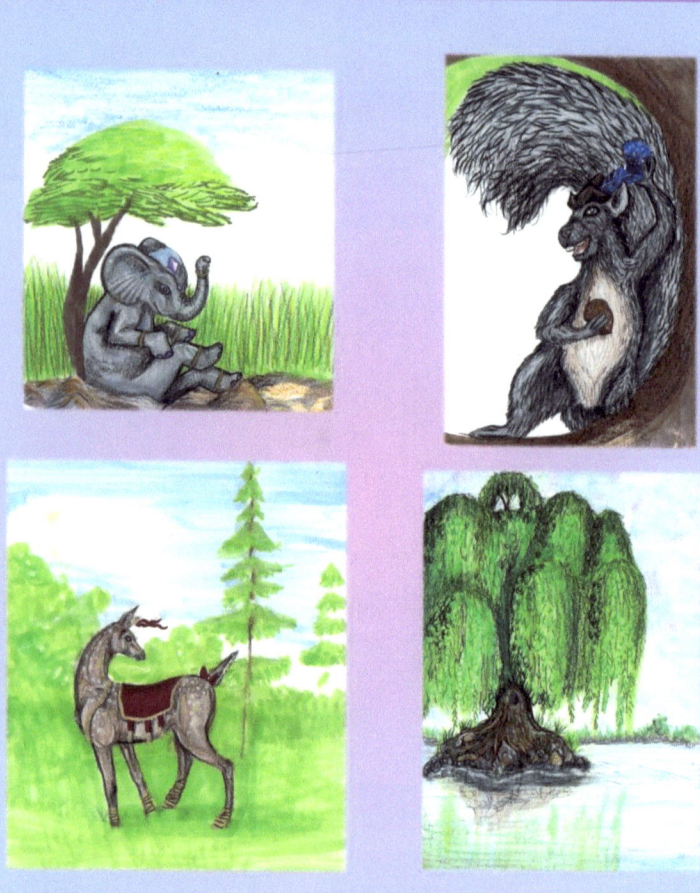

I gain inspiration from the animals and plants I see around me. Sometimes they are quite "natural" looking beings, while other times, I create something completely new. I study anatomy to better help me draw my mythological creatures.

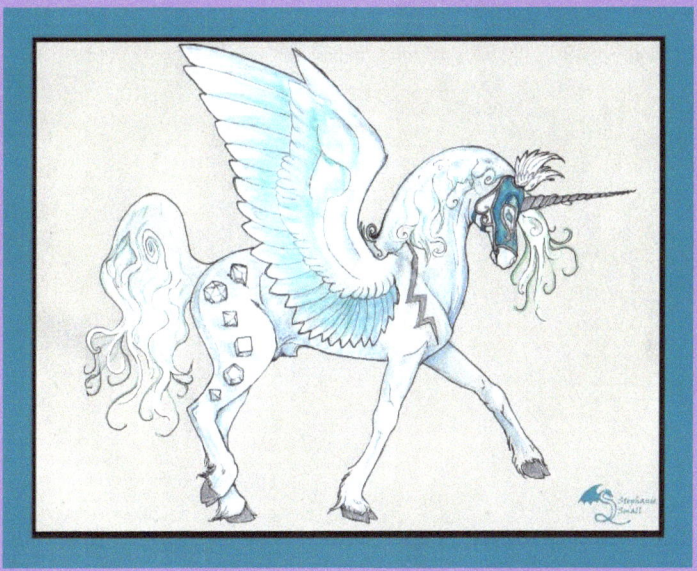
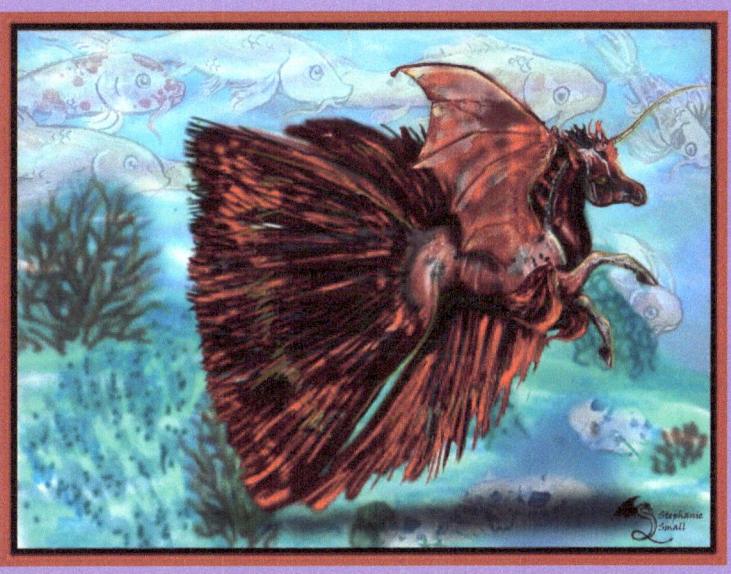

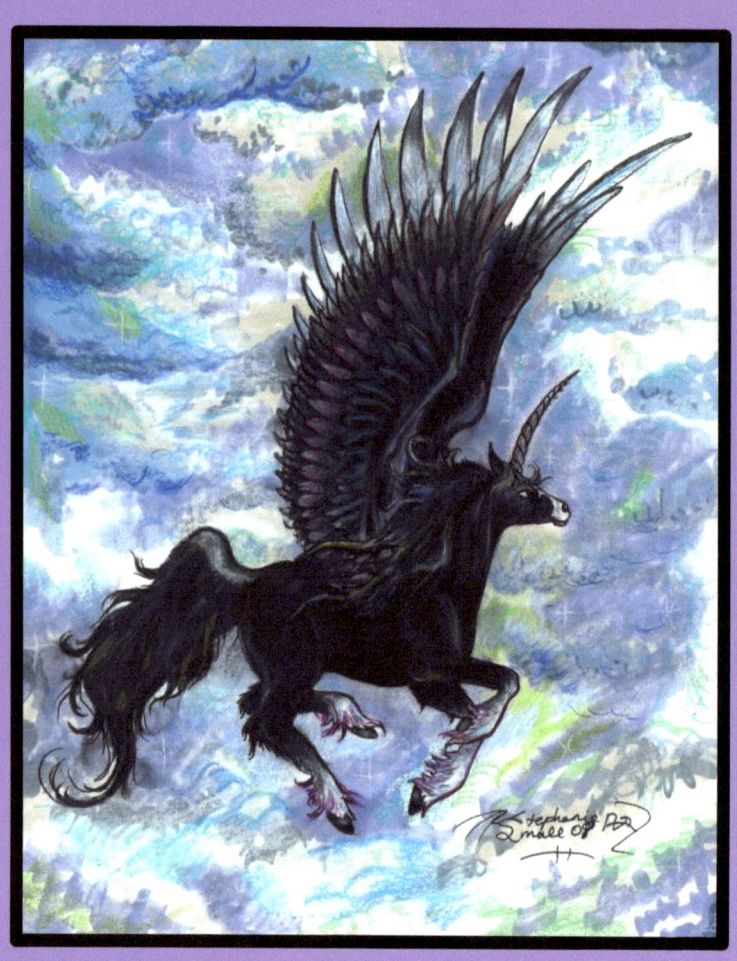

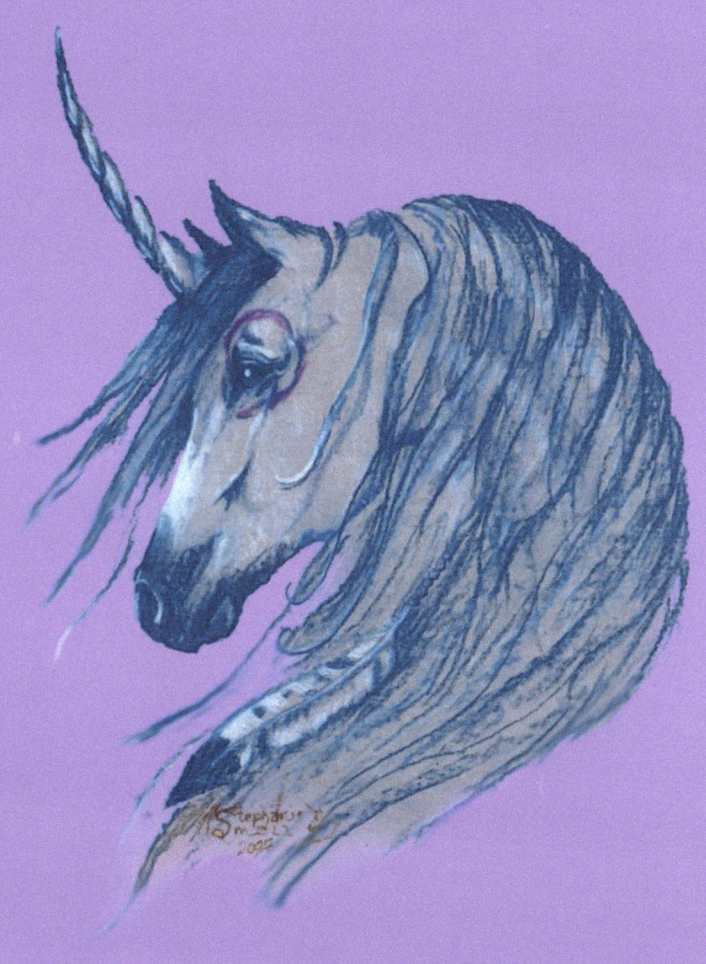

Legends, lore and learning about other religions greatly contributes to the development of art. History, costuming (clothing from different periods) as well as equipment can be a handy way to embellish art.

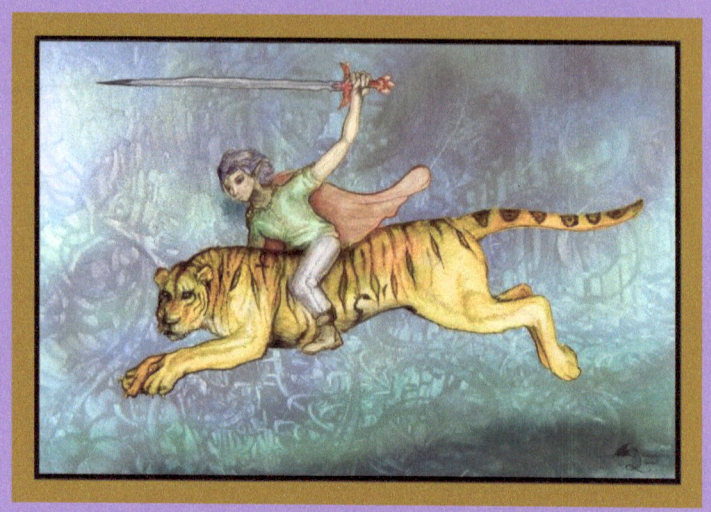

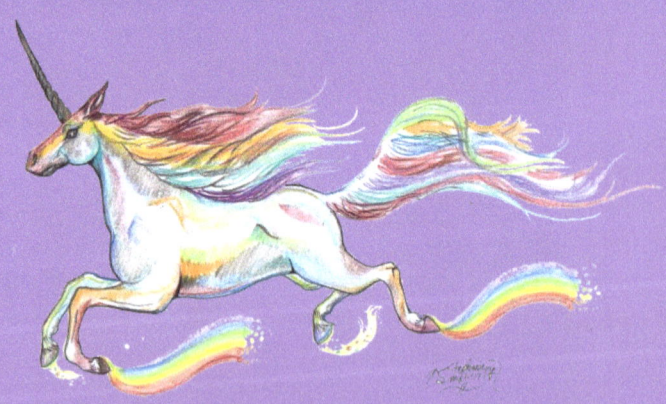

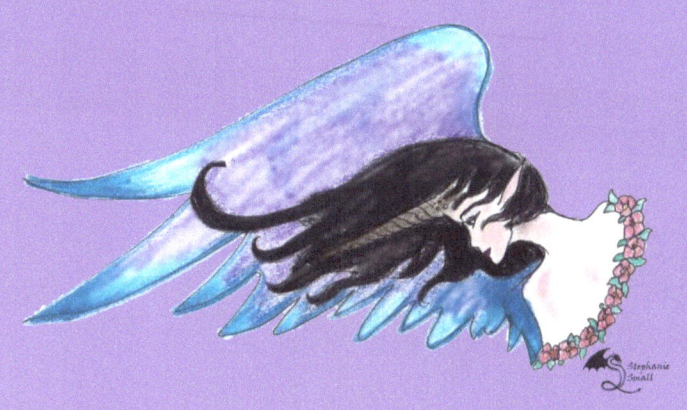

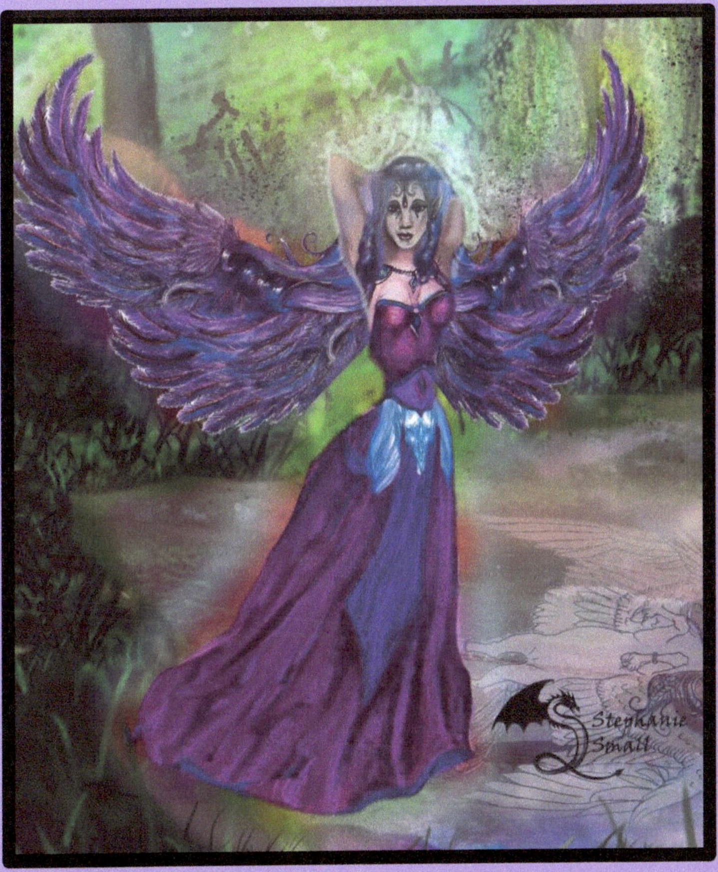

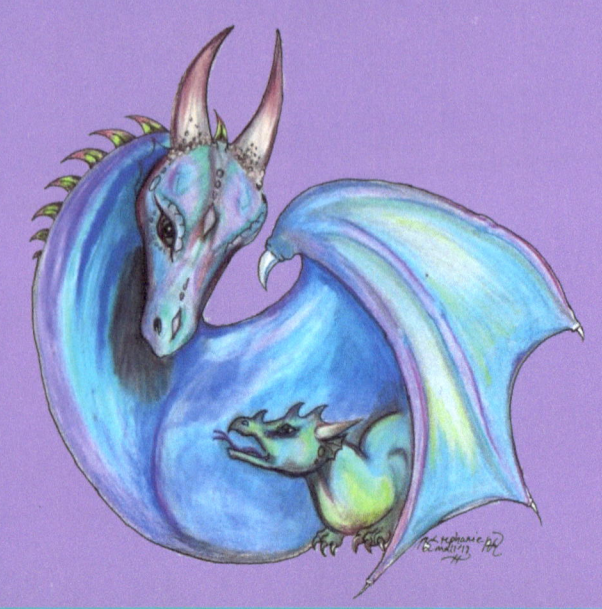
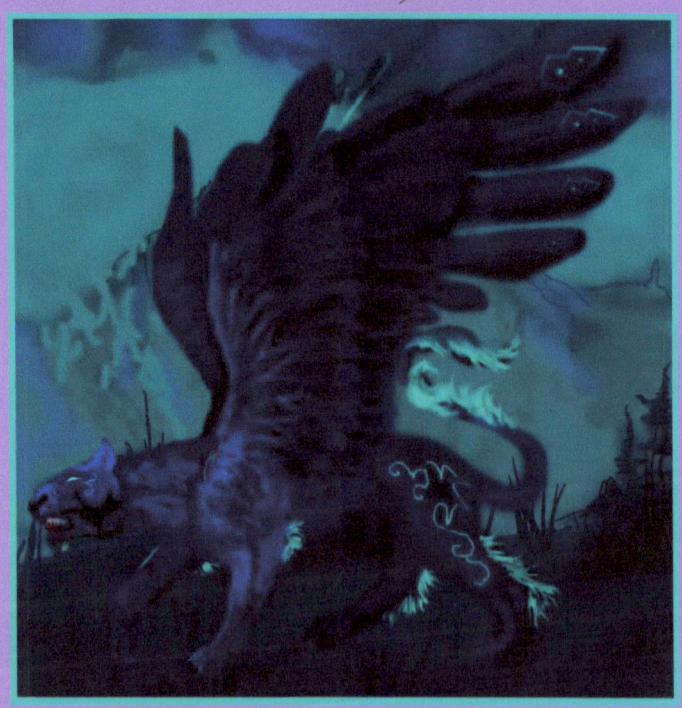

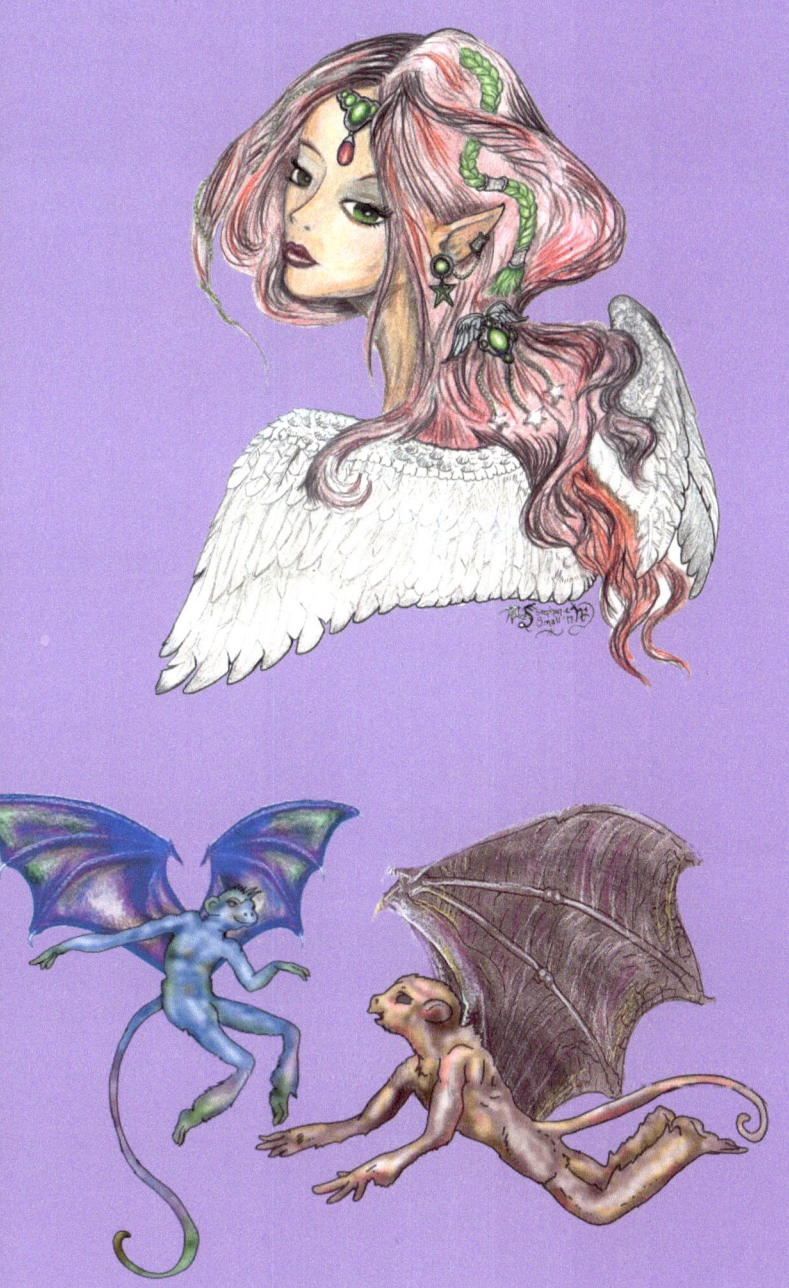

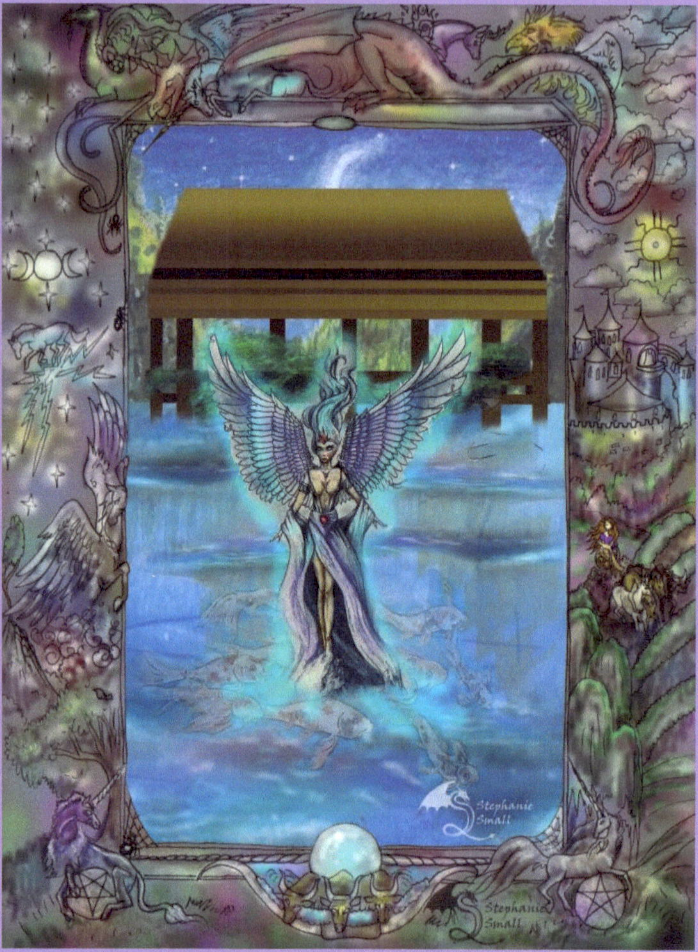

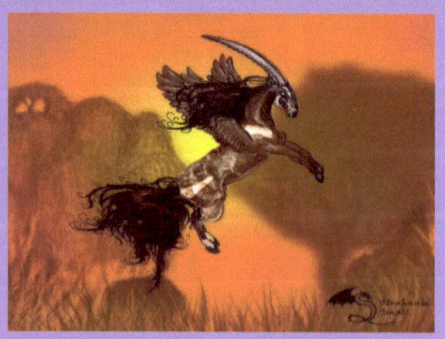

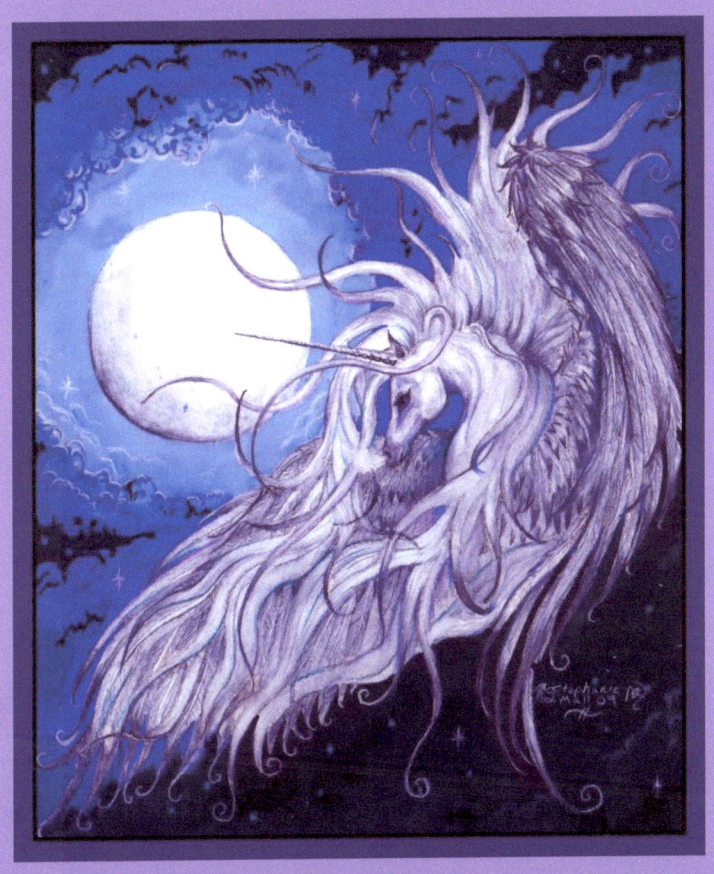

Stephanie Small: About the Author

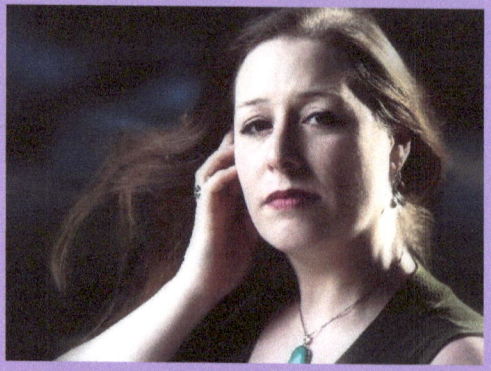

Stephanie Small is an artist and actress located in California. Nature is an influential inspiration to Stephanie, as she seeks to augment and reflect what she sees around her in a variety of mediums. Inspired by medieval art, the fantasy and science fiction genre and more, Stephanie has developed a style of mythical realism.

Stephanie uses a variety of styles and mixed mediums in her artwork. She regularly uses digital mediums such as Photoshop, Illustrator, Painter and more. She favors traditional mediums such as colored pencil, chalk, pen, ink, pencil, acrylic, watercolor. She has been known to adapt fabric, recycled art, recycled purses to create art that is both useful and stylish.

Stephanie has been interviewed and featured in several magazines and websites. Her artwork has been published several times in books and magazines. She is best known for artwork featured in publications such as the Page, the Twisted Vine and the Unicorn.

Stephanie Small is an actress best known for her appearances in 13 Reasons Why (season 2), Antman 2 and other movies.

www.ingramcontent.com/pod-product-compliance
Lightning Source LLC
Chambersburg PA
CBHW040244220526
45473CB00001B/365